The
UNDERCLIFF

The
UNDERCLIFF

A SKETCHBOOK OF THE AXMOUTH – LYME REGIS NATURE RESERVE

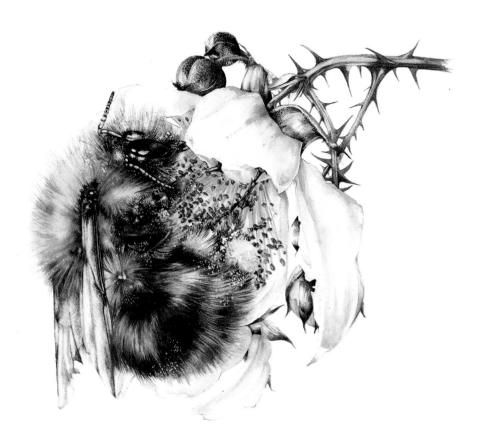

ELAINE FRANKS

Foreword by
JOHN FOWLES

J. M. DENT & SONS LTD
London

For John

J. M. Dent & Sons Ltd
91 Clapham High Street
London SW4 7TA

Produced by
Robert Ditchfield Ltd
Combe Court
Kerry's Gate
Hereford HR2 0AH

First published 1989

Typeset by Action Typesetting Ltd, Gloucester
Printed and bound in Hong Kong

ISBN 0-460-04773-6

HALF TITLE PAGE 10 Spot Ladybird, *Adalia 10 punctata*
TITLE PAGE Bumble Bee, *Bombus agrorum*

CONTENTS

The drawings are arranged by location (please see the map on pages 156–7).

FOREWORD

As a name, the Undercliff is now primarily used, if somewhat loosely, of all that coastal area between Lyme Regis in Dorset and Axmouth in Devon. There are other undercliffs in this cross-county area, for instance in Dorset those of Black Ven and Stonebarrow just east of Lyme, in Devon that of Hooken Cliffs between Seaton and Branscombe to the west. An undercliff is the steep and broken area, made of formerly subsided or still subsiding cliff between the last agricultural land and the sea-shore. Its rich and often luxuriant wild life is caused by three main factors. In the South-west, facing the Channel, it is both tilted towards the sun and protected from cruel north winds. Here in West Dorset and East Devon it is also very well watered; and indeed it is the water, together with the geology – the nature of the soils – that makes this 'greenhouse' land famously (or notoriously) unstable; and gives rise to the third factor, its never having been seriously disturbed by man. Even the most determined farmer or would-be developer has had in the past to think twice about exploiting it; and now it is safely under national protection.

From the sea, on a fine summer's day, the Undercliff is in short a triumphant denial of contemporary reality, an apparent sub-tropical paradise, a Robinson Crusoe landscape that seems at a glance the ruthless developer's dream; not a roof to be seen, not a road, not a sign of man. It looks almost as the world might have been if man had not evolved, so pure, so unspoilt, so untouched it is scarcely credible, so unaccustomed that on occasion its solitudes may feel faintly eery.

It was not always so. Indeed two hundred years ago, the near 800 acres of the Undercliff were probably far less wild than they are now. Much of it was then run with sheep, and grazed as rough pasture. It was also alive with rabbits, now much reduced by myxomatosis; and it has become so heavily covered by trees and undergrowth only in this century. Many old people can still remember an area in the eastern part of the Undercliff called Donkey Green; of picnicking and playing cricket there on the expanse of turf. Today Donkey Green is a formidable jungle-thicket, unimaginably changed, in less than a century, from its former self. Various other favourite Undercliff resorts of the past, Mrs Gapper's Cottage, Whitechapel Rocks (where the persecuted early dissenters went for their secret prayer meetings) and the rest, are now virtually forgotten places, and indeed off the path that the Nature Conservancy Council – for the Undercliff is now mercifully a National Nature Reserve – allows the public to use.

The unthinking or those fierce for common rights may feel this limiting of access to the one path is unfair; but this is above all a *nature* reserve, somewhere where the needs of man are not paramount, as they are over so much of the South-west; but the needs of nature itself. There is also a much more practical reason. Once off the path, one can get lost or – in that vivid Devon dialect word – pixy-led, totally and mysteriously confused, in the Undercliff with a bewildering ease and this is emphatically not country in which not to know where one is going. Local hunts have always anxiously whipped their hounds away if they threaten to go down into it. Much of it is full of small cliffs, often concealed, always insecure at the edge; some of it has very boggy ground. There are pools, dark greenly deep. Covered crevices are ubiquitous. Undergrowth can be nightmarishly dense, penetrable only by the badgers and roe-deer. I once lived in a farm on its border, and the sight of bramble-torn,

View of the Great Chasm of the Axmouth Landslip: Reaping the Wheat 25th August 1840 by William Dawson (courtesy of The Philpot Museum, Lyme Regis)

limping, exhausted tourists, seemingly fresh-emerged from hell, was far from infrequent. Every year the local rescue services are called out to search for or save someone gone astray. People who know it never take the Undercliff lightly. The rule is simple: never leave the main path without permission.

There was a time also when the sheep were often disturbed at night. Smuggling has gone on along this coast for centuries, and was particularly rife at the end of the eighteenth and beginning of the last. One celebrated local rogue, John Rattenbury, nicknamed the Rob Roy of the West, 'cruised' (or smuggled) into both Beer and Lyme, but particularly at Charton Bay between them, a remarkable and still totally deserted strand in the heart of the Undercliff. So many 'free trade' goods passed there, and up to Rousdon and Whitlands, that the Preventive Service had in the end (in 1827) to establish a look-out post at the edge of the inland cliffs.

But perhaps the most remarkable happening in the Undercliff took place at the very end of 1839, when there was a huge landslip. A great slice of the inland cliff below Bindon Manor and Dowlands Farm collapsed, forming what is now known as Goat Island and the Chasm. Part of the fall was of a wheatfield, already sown. It was reaped on August 25th, 1840, and before, so local newspapers said, some 10,000 spectators. Despite its fallen position, this was with great rejoicing. The reapers were led, at least symbolically, by young ladies, who were given silver brooches, in the form of a sickle, as mementoes. For a long time people came from far and wide to view this strange and ominous event, which was extended in 1840, from February on, to the area of Whitlands and Charton Bay, although that received less attention than the first slip at Bindon. One August Sunday in 1867 you might have met three endlessly talking men in the wilderness. One was Francis Palgrave, the famous anthologist, the second was the Irish poet William Allingham; and the third was a far greater poet still, Tennyson. They treasured their ramble, like thousands both before and since.

Local farmers and hotel and lodging-house keepers must have blessed the day the subsidence began. The worthy Mr. Chappell, tenant at the original Dowlands Farm (the present farm was not built until 1847), charged all visitors sixpence each to use his path, an old cart road, down to the event. If that may seem an early instance of a farmer discovering grockles are more profitably cultivated than cereals, it must in fairness be said that the first visitors had severely trampled his crops, and he claimed some compensation was due. At the beginning the cause was widely attributed to an earthquake, although the pioneer geologists William Buckland and Conybeare, both also clergymen, and now the students of the new science of geomorphology, knew and continue to know very well that landslipping in this area is a complex story of undrained water and the permeable and impermeable strata down into which it runs.

Some beds, such as the Jurassic Lias Clay and the Cretaceous Gault, will not let water in; others, such as the overlying Cretaceous Upper Greensand, 'foxmould' in local terms, dissolve before it. The result is rather like removing one in a tall pile of precariously balanced books; the others are fatally upset.

A local farmer once put it ungeologically, but eloquently, to me: 'All this land, 'tis in love with the sea.' That is, it seems permanently eager to tumble down and join it. The sea between Lyme and Axmouth is incidentally nowhere more than 30 feet deep until five or six miles out. If we could see beneath the waves it would be of a huge shelf of previously subsided coast. A very recent and massive subsidence, in the winter of 1986-7 and continued through that of 1987-8, took place just east of Lyme in the National Trust land above the Spittals; and one can gain from that some idea of the terrible (to human minds) consequences of these frightening and frequent occurrences on this coast – peaceful meadows turned in a few weeks (landslipping is rarely an instantaneous, cataclysmic event but much more a long-echoing one) to 1914-18 battlefields, horrors of riven ground and uprooted trees. Nature itself adapts better, especially the plants. Two uncommon and beautiful orchids of this area, the Bee and the Marsh Helleborine, seem actually to benefit from these regular upheavals. It is why, in good years, they are not uncommon. But the 1839-40 Landslip gave the nervous of early Victorian England a grave shock, and the stern moralists a pleasing theme; God, it seemed, was in a rage with sinful man.

The Undercliff is today, so far less religion-cowed, a most happy sanctuary, a secret Mecca for natural historians and geologists, a delight for ordinary nature – and landscape – lovers. I treasure it myself for its solitudes, its silences, its sheer beauty, its exuberance of growth, its memories of very different pasts and cultures. It is for me not primarily a fascinating area geologically, or a wonderful nature reserve, but quite simply one of those places one always thinks of as one does of a poem or piece of music; not quite of this world; or, of this world as it should be, but alas so largely isn't.

When we were filming *The French Lieutenant's Woman* in it, the film crew, struggling with manhandling impossible weights over very rough ground indeed, fighting the endless difficulties of communication and supply (and light – don't make films under eternal canopies of trees), had a tee-shirt printed. Across its chest ran I HATE THE UNDERCLIFF. I understood their particular reasons, but for me it summed up a large part of what is wrong with our world. Haters of the Undercliff – and all it stands for – are lost in a way even the most foolish literal wanderers there are not. Increasingly modern man cannot face ancient and untamed nature like this; where nature itself, the elements, rule, not man; where iron and concrete and plastic are powerless; where it defeats all use except enjoyment on its own terms. That is why we have lost so much, and are now lost ourselves; and why I welcome this charming reminder of what is hidden there. The Undercliff is indeed a lost place; but most profoundly, the lost place is in ourselves.

John Fowles

INTRODUCTION

The landslip between Axmouth and Lyme Regis is impenetrable and unstable territory, and the only way of getting through is by following the path maintained by the Nature Conservancy Council. It is simply not a place for human beings – even less so now than in the past. But for wildlife this means it is a sanctuary. Animals and plants are much happier coping with the shifting ground and crashing cliffs than with the total clearance that is required when land is developed; and the range of habitats is remarkable – cliff-face, dense woodland, fresh-water ponds, open, rocky scrub, sea shore.

It is the creatures and plants of these habitats that are the subject of this book, but the conditions in which they thrive present the illustrator with several problems. An A2 board, let alone all the other equipment needed for a piece of finished artwork, is a cumbersome object to carry for four miles in a landscape that can be hard to negotiate at the best of times. Away from the path that winds through the Reserve, you invariably find it impossible to balance yourself and materials at the ideal viewpoint. Pens and pencils slide down crevices or get dropped in the undergrowth and are hidden for ever.

So there is no question of producing paintings or even finished sketches in the wild. This is essentially a place for gathering impressions and information, and for this I need equipment that will help me observe and record things quickly – binoculars, a camera and a small notebook. In the book I scribble my observations, thumb-nail sketches, map references and weather conditions – a wealth of impressions and details that it would take me years to get down directly onto the drawing board. Some of these notes are supported by photographs, particularly if the subject is static, like a plant or slow-moving insect. I use a 28-200 mm zoom lens on an aged Pentax body with good results in light conditions, but less so in gloomier areas of the Undercliff, where an ancient f1.8 55mm lens is excellent; a x2 converter for those far-away moments (often used with a monopod converted from one of my husband's old cymbal stands); and a set of extension tubes for insects and details of plants. A 400 ASA film gives me the range to achieve an adequate depth of field under most, but not all, conditions.

Armed thus with notebook, camera and binoculars, I quietly watch and listen, aiming to merge into the landscape and absorb the surrounding images, smells and sounds. Sometimes it can be a cold, wet business, but there is no way round that; you have to be a part of it and get cold and wet along with everyone else.

The easiest things to observe are those you can get close to – insects, for example. I have found that being very short-sighted has helped me to appreciate insects. When I was a child, birds were those dark things that always seemed to be out of focus, but a wasp busy at a pool of jam was a delight – the fascinating complexity of its structure and actions, the exquisite detail of its markings. As for butterflies, I could sit with my nose in a clump of Michaelmas daisies for hours, watching them uncurl their delicate hairspring tongues to feed. Now that my eyes have slowed their myopic decline, I can see the distant world clearly and have discovered the joys of bird-watching, but I still have a particular fascination with insects. Far more numerous and varied than other types of fauna, they are often dismissed as no more than nuisances – 'creepy-crawlies' – to be swatted or doused in pesticide. If not slaughtered, they are generally overlooked or treated with disdain. Yet I know of no

Elaine Franks sketching in the Undercliff (photograph by John Franks)

richer colour than the electric green of a shiny-backed fly basking in the sun, or construction more impressive than the precision engineering of a beetle. To me, each insect seems a minute miracle. Yes, they can be a nuisance and bite or sting, but so would I if something the size of Everest tried to sit on me.

I find reptiles and amphibians nearly as remarkable as insects. They are another group of animals which tend to arouse inherited phobias in people. I hope that my paintings of both these and insects will transmit my enthusiasm for them and do them some service with the only species that can really appreciate their beauty.

Trying to sketch more mobile animals in the Undercliff requires great patience and different techniques. On cliffs or open land I can often draw while observing a subject closely through a pair of binoculars mounted on a tripod. This has proved impossible in the Undercliff; a bird may be in view for only a second or two as it flies between trees, and the fractured scenery makes it virtually impossible to follow the quarry. To overcome this problem, I try to use my eyes as a camera, to 'take' an image and keep it in my head, putting down as many details of jizz, coloration and lighting as I can before it fades. Often when I am painting, the moment will be revived by these notes; the piece then becomes more and more of a struggle as I try to translate the incident into one inadequate plane.

The green woodpecker on page 107 typifies the sketching problem. During a period of some thirty minutes I had heard the bird's laughing yaffle, but had been unable to spot it. Whilst I was making notes about a dog-rose, a movement drew my eye away – the woodpecker bounced up from the ground and dodged behind a tree trunk. I looked for it, searching the tree. There – higher than before. For half a second the bird was still, planning its next move; then it was gone. Taking my notes to Exeter Museum, I handled skins and mounts, learning the form and structure of the bird. I began to build up the framework for the painting, taking colour notes and making drawings of details such as the beak and feet. At home a couple of photographs from my files showed me what the bird would be doing with its feet. Back on the drawing board all these fragments were worked together into the completed painting.

I have time to observe only a small fraction of what is happening in the life cycle of each species. Museums, books, my own files of notes, sketches and photographs, even radio and television programmes can help me to learn more about their lives, behaviour, history and the context in which they live. These things are a part of their fascination, and for this reason I have added notes and observations to the illustrations in this book.

I am better able to draw an animal if I know its structure, and collect any skeletons or dead animals I come across for my own 'mini-museum'. Some of these are illustrated in the following pages. Preparing skeletons is rather a fiddly business, but well worth the effort involved. I find the best way is to bury the corpses in a clearly labelled container of garden soil. At one time I put the bodies straight into the garden, but after losing several, including a magnificent tawny owl of which I was only ever able to find one leg, I had to organize the process a little differently. Although much depends on the soil and weather conditions, something the size of a squirrel will generally take four to five months to decompose, a mole about six weeks and a woodmouse about three weeks. After a suitable period of time, the pot is emptied out onto a sheet of black polythene, and then comes the fiddly bit – working through the soil (now crumbly and darker in colour) picking out the skull and as many bones as possible, washing them and sticking them onto a card. I find skulls particularly useful as, once the head is positioned as I want, the rest of the animal becomes much easier to draw. When picked over, the soil is returned to my garden to benefit the plants, quite a few of which form a living 'library' of native species.

After all this preparatory work come the illustrations. I must somehow depict on paper the life that I have seen in the wild. The photographs I have taken are, like the written notes and sketches, a jog to the memory; I never copy a photograph. Nor do I work from other people's illustrations. I find real pleasure in the research and the hundreds of discoveries I make in just a day's work in the wild, so it makes no sense to limit the subjects of pictures to those chosen by another illustrator. But I have, of course, learnt a lot from other people, and from looking at the work of the great artists of the past.

The first drawings that I remember being excited by were Dürer's studies of plants and animals. I was, I believe, about eight or nine at the time and I remember wishing I could draw like that. A few years later, on a trip to London, I saw two paintings by Richard Dadd which, like the Dürer drawings, have stayed with me. I was impressed by the detail, the idea that nothing was too small to be seen and painted, that there was indeed a separate world at the base of grass stems. Later came Samuel Palmer. All the grubbing around under bushes had led to my being totally clueless about how to approach landscape; I would end up with a couple of detailed grass stems in one corner of a large sheet of paper, or would find myself trying to draw every leaf on a tree. Whilst at college, I had seen and fallen in love with Palmer's 'magical' landscapes, but when I found a wide cross-section of his work in a biography, it was like a key turning in a very rusty lock – my wonder at his paintings was rekindled, and for the first time I saw his sketches and drawings and began to understand how I might be able to approach landscape.

While I wonder at the creation I see around me, I remain a realist and have no wish to be a painter of pretty, tidied up, sanitized pictures of nature as many people would like it to be. Nature is not 'nice'. You will find, for example, that many butterflies have tatty wings, for one reason or another. That is their life, that is how they are. There are some tatty butterflies in this book, but none the less beautiful for that.

Because I like to reproduce animals and plants in fine detail (doubtless, again, a result of my short-sightedness) I need a very hard paper with a smooth texture to work on. Rough paper means less detail and fine effects are more difficult to create. I mainly use Schoelleshammer paper, and once I have stretched it find I can do almost anything I want – sometimes sanding it, sometimes cutting into it with a sharp knife.

I apply watercolours from pans in a variety of ways: straight washes, dry brush, wet onto wet, dry onto wet, spattered with toothbrush or diffuser, sponged, catching the edge of a rich pool of watercolour with a brush loaded with clean water, washing out areas once they have dried. The possiblities of watercolour seem unlimited – it is an amazing medium. Some pigments are incompatible, with the result that they will settle out in different areas of a wash; or they have different dye strengths, so that you can lay down a dense wash of, say, blue-green, leave it to dry, then lift out bits of it with clean water and tissue to give areas of bright yellow green. For textures like rock, earth or moss, I can achieve a granular effect by sprinkling suitable sizes of salt grains onto a wash and then brushing it off when competely dry. A strong saline solution also makes an interesting network of veins in a wash. Paint printed from the edge of a piece of thin card can help with grass and other linear plants, and even thumb-prints have their uses. Highlights are either washed, scraped and masked out or added on top with gouache or pencil – coloured pencil on dark watercolour can give a lovely sheen to the back of a beetle.

Each spread in this book has been executed with a variety of materials – watercolour primarily, but also pencil (from H to 6B), coloured pencil (hard and soft), coloured inks, wax, gouache etc. I often finish a piece with watercolour varnish, this being necessary to bring out the jewel-like qualities that may have been lost when layers of dark watercolour have dried and become duller in the process.

Such techniques are never an end in themselves. They are a means of presenting a scene with immediacy. What I have tried to do is use them to convey the intense beauty of these wild things, living in this extraordinary place, untouched by the twentieth century.

Elaine Franks

13

Once when I entered the lane to the Undercliff I came across a cluster of red-legged partridges browsing on the surrounding vegetation. They seemed nervous, glancing around to check for danger. Apparently I presented them with a major threat for on catching sight of me they scuttled off down the green lane and disappeared into a field.

Another unexpected species, *Lamium variegatum* — a garden plant that may have arrived by local people tipping garden refuse.

The stile makes a good seat
for butterfly-watching. Many common
hedgerow species in evidence here —
small tortoiseshells, skippers,
red admirals, small coppers,
gate-keepers and an early
peacock or two. The
one that catches my
eye is a large bright
yellow butterfly that has a
relaxed way of flying as it
moves from flower to flower, always closing
its wings as it comes to rest —
the brimstone
(*Gonepteryx rhamni*).

1. the eggs
are laid
singly

2. and hatch after
about ten days.

the
larvae
feed on
buckthorn

3. One month after hatching,
the fifth instar
pupates; the butterfly emerges after about
a fortnight.

brimstone
emerging
from its
pupa

Stripe-winged Grasshopper
(stenobothrus lineatus) x4

Great Green Bush-cricket ♀
(Tettigonia viridissima)
x1·25
Active from mid-day onwards,
late July to
mid-oct.

Greenfinch ♂
lifesize,
still showing brighter
breeding plumage.

Greenfinches have increased in number in recent
years in the Undercliff. They can be seen in flocks in the
lane and woodland margins above the slip, but are seldom
found in the thicker growth of the Undercliff.

16mm

The heavy beak shows that they are well equipped to deal with
tough-coated seeds and nuts.

In open country the bird has a
distinctive bouncing flight, given by a
pattern of several wingbeats followed by a
brief spell with wings closed.

Flint-strewn fields cover the hills at the top of the slip – with many familiar calcareous plants along their margins; the clover and vetch families and bird's-foot trefoil, which is one of the larval food plants of the Common Blue butterfly, a minutely patterned jewel of an insect.

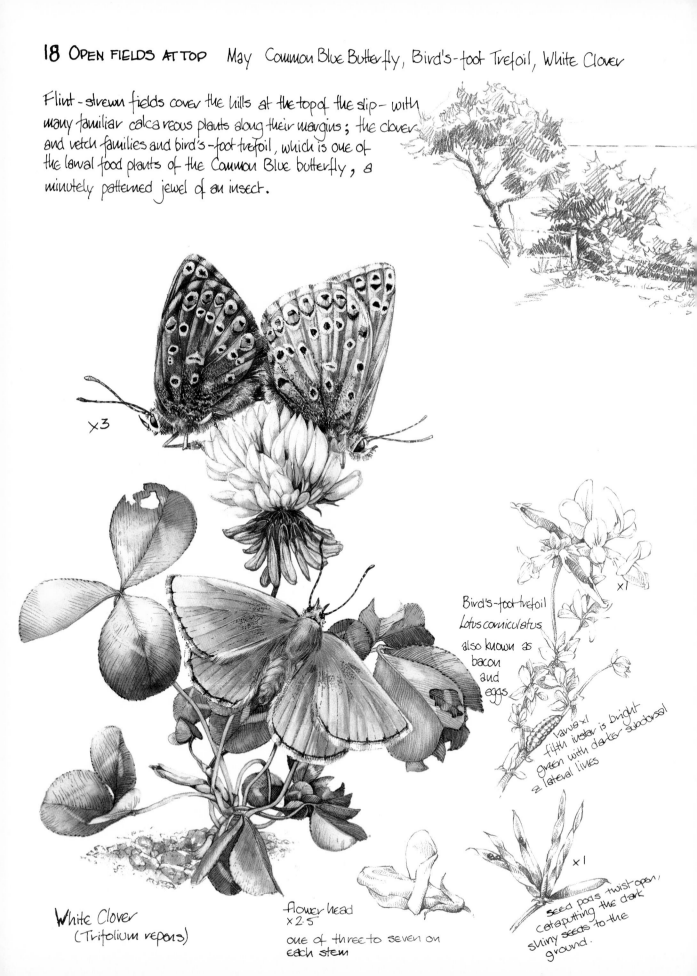

x3

Bird's-foot trefoil
Lotus corniculatus

also known as
bacon
and
eggs

×1

larva ×1
fifth instar is bright
green with darker subdorsal
& lateral lines

×1

seed pods twist open,
catapulting the dark
shiny seeds to the
ground.

White Clover
(*Trifolium repens*)

flower head
×2·5

one of three to seven on
each stem

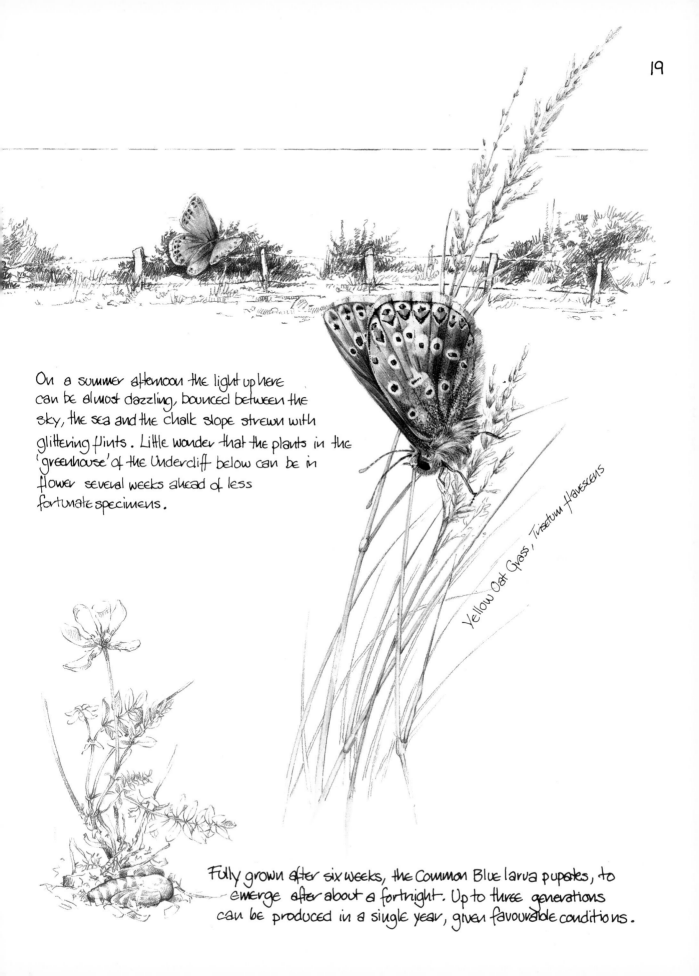

On a summer afternoon the light up here
can be almost dazzling, bounced between the
sky, the sea and the chalk slope strewn with
glittering flints. Little wonder that the plants in the
'greenhouse' of the Undercliff below can be in
flower several weeks ahead of less
fortunate specimens.

Yellow Oat Grass, Trisetum flavescens

Fully grown after six weeks, the Common Blue larva pupates, to
emerge after about a fortnight. Up to three generations
can be produced in a single year, given favourable conditions.

20 BINDON June Stonechat

The western extremity of the Reserve; it was just east of this point that the great slip of 1839 occurred, forming the features now known as Goat Island and the Chasm. On Christmas night 1839 the coast guards on duty heard noises 'resembling the rending of cloth' — the ground shook beneath them, great cracks opening up beneath their feet, off Culverhole point they saw a great land mass rising from the sea. The slip left a great chasm inland, some three quarters of a mile long, 150 feet deep and 250 feet wide.

Part of the ground which had slipped had previously been sown with wheat which continued to grow and in due course ripened. An engraving in the Philpot Museum at Lyme commemorates the

festivities surrounding the harvesting of this
crop on 25th August 1840. A crowd of some 6,000
onlookers - a local band plays martial music as the
Committee leads the procession wearing blue 'ribands'
around their necks. Then come six young lady
reapers - The Nymphs of Ceres - wearing white
kid gloves, carrying wreaths of artificial
flowers and sickles adorned with blue
ribbons. Lastly six
gentlemen resplendent in
blue vests and white trousers.
The nymphs were not skilled
reapers, one of them succeeded
in cutting her hand at the first
stroke of her sickle and her
companions soon tired —
the task was handed over
to the professionals.

Stonechat - often
seen perched on
top of bushes in
this area

Bombus lucorum ♀ ×8

At this time of year Bindon is abuzz with
bees. Several species may be found on the
south-facing slopes. The largest and easiest
to spot are the bumble bees.

Andrena haemorrhoa ♀
×1

Bombus terrestris ♀
×·75

Anthidium
manicatum ×1
♂

Toadflax
(*Linaria vulgaris*)
and Hedge Bedstraw
(*Galium mollugo*) —
both lifesize.
Only bees with a long proboscis
(like the bumble bee, but not the honey
bee) can reach the nectar in
spurred flowers like the toadflax.

At the base of a clump of grasses, a remnant of skin, perhaps from a buzzard's meal, shows that adders are present here. Bindon must be an ideal habitat for the adder as it has a plentiful supply of its food species — mice, voles, shrews, slow worms, lizards — and provides a south facing, scrub-covered slope for basking in the sun. Despite its reputation, the adder is not an aggressive creature, always preferring 'flight' to 'fight' in its encounters with human beings. It will, however, defend itself if it must and should always be treated with respect and caution.

poison fang

lower jaw

the curved teeth point down the throat

A number of chalk-loving plants can be found in open patches between larger scrub species, such as gorse and blackthorn. Some of them colonize the bare chalk left by small slides.

Thyme
(Thymus serpyllum agg.)

Others scramble up over the tangles of bramble and scrub.

Yet others intermingle with the shorter grasses.

Tufted Vetch
(Vicia cracca)

Milkwort
(Polygala vulgaris)

This place always puts me in mind of a vast overgrown rock garden. A tumble of rocks
and boulders supports a wide variety of summer colour, great trails of pink everlasting
pea and white field rose, the rich purple-blue of self-heal, the flame colours of ripening
wayfaring tree fruits. It was here that I once saw a surprisingly early butterfly: Feb.12th
was a magical day that came after a seemingly unending period of wind, snow and rain.
Bindon appeared as if set apart from the grim grey of the surrounding countryside,
a special place of warmth with a golden light softly reflected from the cliffs at the back

of the ledge. I had unpeeled layers of now unnecessary water proofing and was sitting with my back against a comfortable rock soaking up this wonderful and unexpected warmth, when a butterfly settled on a bramble not two metres away – a red admiral, one of the few that survive our cold winters to emerge in the early spring. It was surely too early to have been a migrant.

The warm weather has brought an early brood of cinnabar caterpillars two or three weeks before I would have expected them. Soon there won't be much left of the ragwort (Senecio jacobaea). Both ragwort and groundsel (another food plant for the cinnabar) are rich in alkaloid poisons. These accumulate in the body of the caterpillar in a form that does not harm it and provide a good deterrent to birds. (They quickly learn of the caterpillars' unpleasant taste and leave them alone.) The poisons are not dispersed, but are carried on through all the stages of growth — caterpillar, chrysalis and moth — giving the species excellent protection against virtually all insectivores.

x4

Cinnabar Moth
(Tyria jacobaeae)

x1·5

x1.5

x2

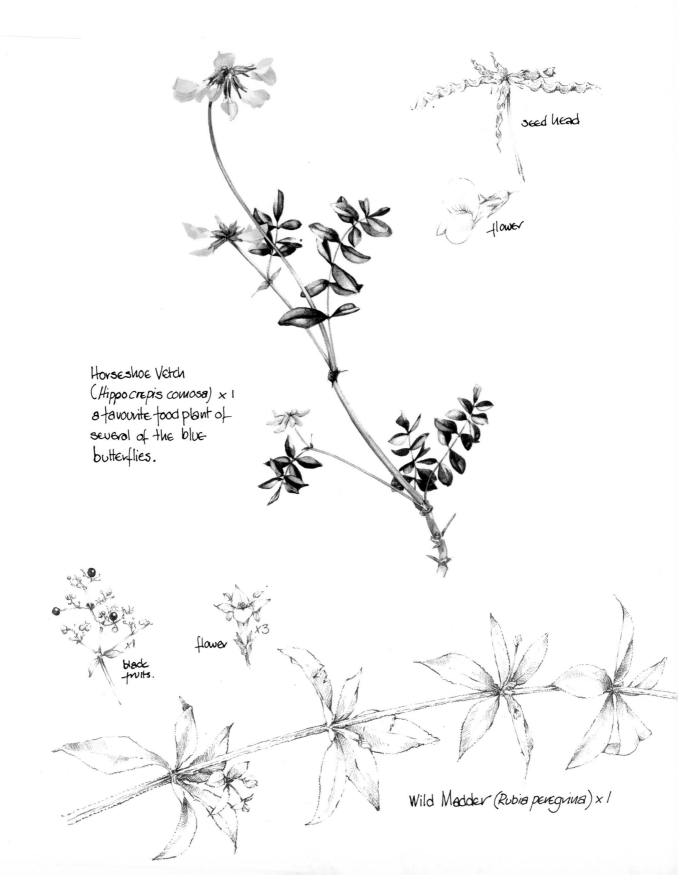

seed head

flower

Horseshoe Vetch
(*Hippocrepis comosa*) x 1
a favourite food plant of
several of the blue
butterflies.

black
fruits.

flower x3

Wild Madder (*Rubia peregrina*) x 1

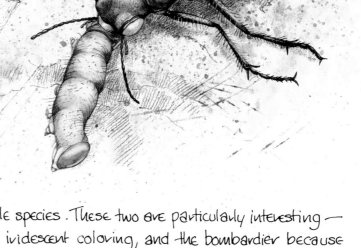

Green Tiger Beetle
(Cicindela campestris) (x5)

Bindon is home for many beetle species. These two are particularly interesting — the tiger beetle because of its iridescent coloring, and the bombardier because of the extraordinary way it deters predators. It ejects a jet of caustic liquid from its anus with explosive force which immediately vaporizes, looking like a small puff of smoke.

Bombardier Beetle
(Brachinus crepitans) x4

Wild Madder — grows vigorously throughout Bindon & other parts of the Undercliff Dyer's madder *(Rubia tinctoria)* is cultivated in southern Europe for the scarlet dye, extracted from its roots.

Strawberries flower here from late March to August — from June onwards both flowers and fruit are found together on the plants.

Wild strawberries may be small, but have a lot of flavour — they thrive in the 'rock garden' here, benefiting from the light and heat reflected from the surrounding rocks and the cliff at the back of the shelf.

x 1

x 1

x 1

spreads by seed & runners, each plant producing up to five of these from its base. Grows outwards until the tip reaches a pocket of soil and takes root, producing new plant.

Common lizard
(*Lacerta vivipara*) ♀ x 1·25

Binoculars are essential when watching lizards. The slightest vibration will cause them to dart away into the cover of undergrowth.. They have a quite distinctive pattern to their daily activity; emerging relatively late, about 9·00 or 10·00 a.m. (presumably when the ground has warmed up a little), they spend the day alternately basking and feeding until early dusk. For the last hour or so, they maximize the sun's heat by basking on rocks that slope towards the sun.

Viviparous lizards very variable in colour — from sandy brown to olive green.

Markings also vary greatly in their boldness and colour

Shy, a retiring and secretive bird which seldom goes to ground, preferring
to stay under cover. From this description you might have expected to see
a sober brown bird, camouflaged to merge with its surroundings. But this
is the bullfinch, the raider of orchards, surely one of the most handsome of birds.
The cock's plumage is quite at odds with his shy habits and is perhaps one of the
reasons for them, such a brilliant coloration giving him little protective camouflage.
When he does emerge, he is a glorious sight – his mango-pink breast and black and
grey markings seem quite appropriate to the lushness of the Undercliff, enhancing
its exotic air.

8.am 23rd October –
A very frosty morning, wing
tips & tail sticking out from a
ball of fluff.

3.pm 2nd December
Male & female feeding on
honeysuckle berries.
The berries are ripped off, crushed
& then rotated between the tongue &
bill to feed off the kernel

Wiping bill on branch to
clean away debris.

2nd May –
Its bud nobbling time!

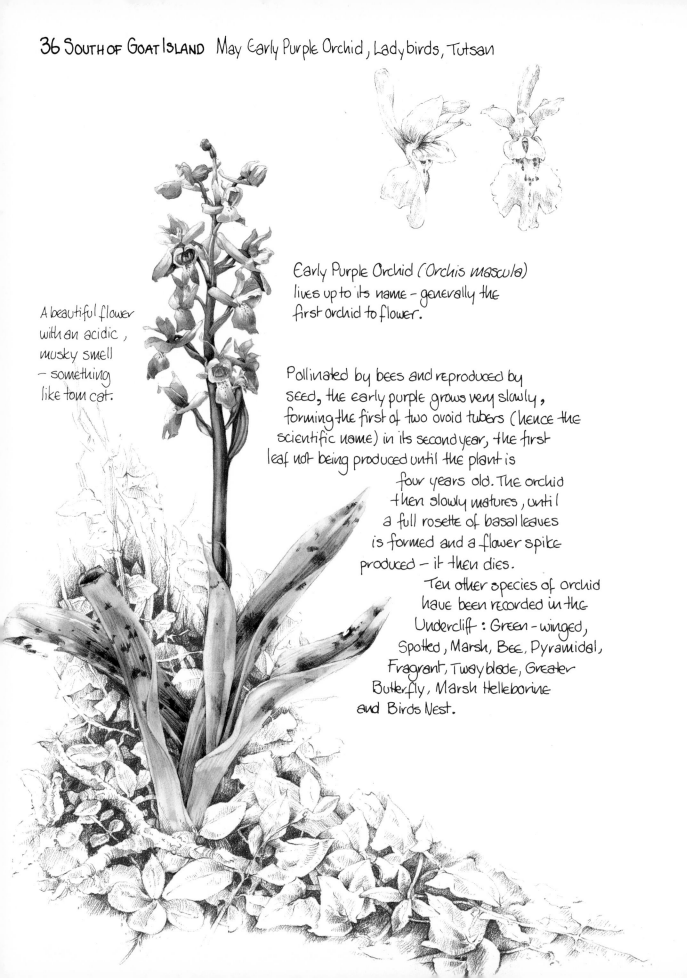

Early Purple Orchid (*Orchis mascula*)
lives up to its name – generally the
first orchid to flower.

A beautiful flower
with an acidic,
musky smell
– something
like tom cat.

Pollinated by bees and reproduced by
seed, the early purple grows very slowly,
forming the first of two ovoid tubers (hence the
scientific name) in its second year, the first
leaf not being produced until the plant is
four years old. The orchid
then slowly matures, until
a full rosette of basal leaves
is formed and a flower spike
produced – it then dies.
Ten other species of orchid
have been recorded in the
Undercliff: Green-winged,
Spotted, Marsh, Bee, Pyramidal,
Fragrant, Twayblade, Greater
Butterfly, Marsh Helleborine
and Birds Nest.

Warfare in the undergrowth!
A sight to make any
gardener happy —
aphids being eaten
by the hundred

Tutsan or Sweet
Amber
(Hypericum
androsaemum). Aromatic
leaves. The name derives
from the Norman 'toute-saine' all heal.

1. Mating under
a leaf.

Some of the
species found
in the
Undercliff

×3

7 spot one of the most
familiar and constant in
appearance

2. Over 30 minute period, ♀ laid 9 pale
yellow eggs on red campion
— about another 191 to come.
These hatch in about 7 days

10 spot, green variety is
shown on
p.108

24 spot — this species
almost never has 24 spots,
generally 16-20. It is
also a vegetarian, feeding
on leguminous plants.

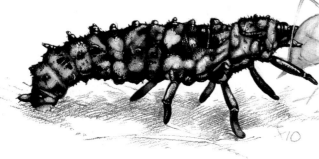

3. Larvae are particularly voracious,
consuming up to 50 aphids per
day — around 1050 in total
before pupating.

4.
4th instar, larva
ready for pupation,
larval skin splits

5.
At first, pupa
still capable of
movement

6.
Soon hardens,
becoming immobile

7. Pupa splits after approx. 7 days, pale adult
struggles free. Rests close to pupal shell approx. 1 hour,
body hardening and drying before capable of flight.
Markings appear within first few hours, but a
day or two before red coloration
develops — derived
from food perhaps?

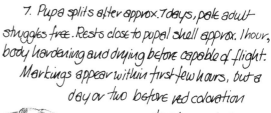 

Walking back along the path as the light was fading, I disturbed a
weasel that had just
killed some small
mammal, a vole I believe.
The first instant I saw it, the
weasel was hunched over its prey,
teeth buried in the back of the neck. It didn't drop
its meal when it saw me, but shifted its grip further
down the animal's back and bounded a few yards
along the path, then off into the undergrowth.

broken claw

×2

normally the
footprints overlap
front & rear, due to the
bounding gait of the animal — but in
some damp mud a few inches from the
scene of the struggle, one remains
distinct. The tip of one claw appears
to be broken.

five flowers arranged in
'town hall clock' fashion

the plant seems
to have a stale
smell

The five-faced Moschatel, or
Town Hall Clock (Adoxa moschatellina)) —
a very fragile-looking plant.

Gladdon much in evidence here.
The first of the peculiar flowers
are now out. Looked at individually,
they have a form that is every bit as
beautiful as any of our garden irises.
The name 'Stinking Iris' has always seemed
a misnomer to me, the smell of the crushed
leaves reminding me far more of cooking meat and
making the other common name — 'Roast Beef Plant'
rather more appropriate.

Like the squirrel, the wood mouse lays up a store of food for the winter, and at this time of the year empty husks from these winter food caches can occasionally be found scattered around nest sites.

Woodmouse tails are apparently very fragile. This mouse had lost all but 1.5cm of his.

Complete skulls can often be found in owl pellets.

×1

The wood mouse is almost entirely nocturnal, as its large eyes show, but it is easily tempted to a regular supply of food. This makes it one of the easier mammals to watch. It is, in fact, the commonest mammal here; the chief food of tawny owls.

From February to early summer the calling and
drumming of woodpeckers may be heard in the
Undercliff. Here at Goat Island the dense
liana-hung woodland must provide them with a
plentiful supply of wood-boring larvae and
nest sites.

It is unusual to catch sight of a Great Spotted Woodpecker, but the fortunate bird-watcher may glimpse one flying between trees in search of food, its red-splashed black and white plumage marking it out. In broken sunlight, however, seeing these birds is not so easy when the eye is dazzled by the many shafts and specks of light. Under these conditions, the black and white plumage gives an element of camouflage to the bird.

A rare sight, a wood white
patrols a small clearing, hovering
like a moth seen in slow motion, its
tremulous flight surely one of the
slowest of all butterflies.

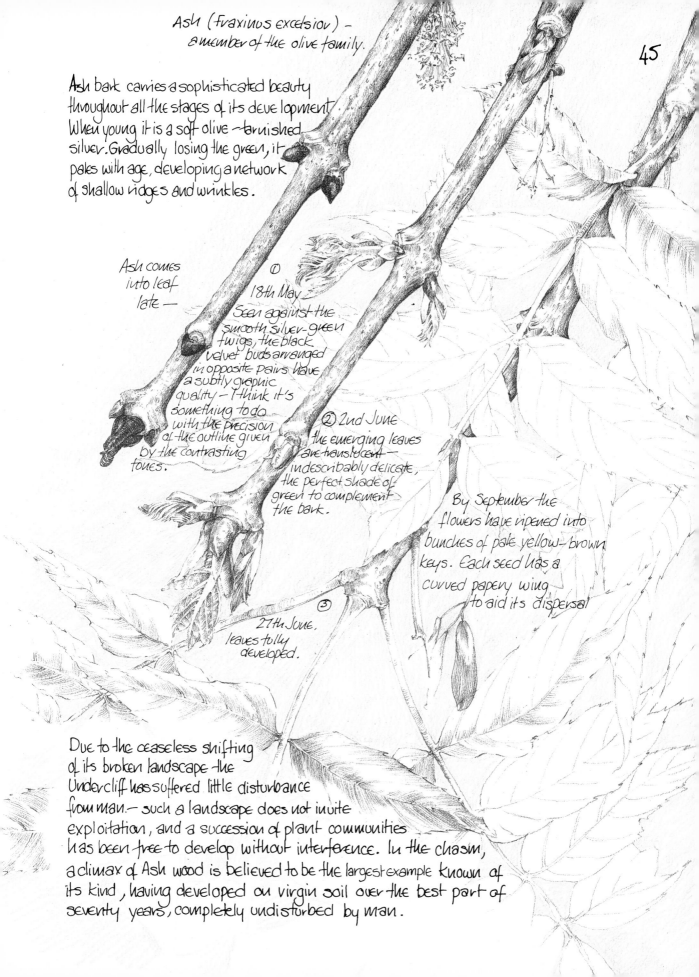

Ash (fraxinus excelsior) –
a member of the olive family.

Ash bark carries a sophisticated beauty
throughout all the stages of its development.
When young it is a soft olive–tarnished
silver. Gradually losing the green, it
pales with age, developing a network
of shallow ridges and wrinkles.

Ash comes
into leaf
late –

① 18th May
Seen against the
smooth silver-green
twigs, the black
velvet buds arranged
in opposite pairs have
a subtly graphic
quality – I think it's
something to do
with the precision
of the outline given
by the contrasting
tones.

② 2nd June
the emerging leaves
are translucent –
indescribably delicate,
the perfect shade of
green to complement
the bark.

③ 27th June,
leaves fully
developed.

By September the
flowers have ripened into
bunches of pale yellow–brown
keys. Each seed has a
curved papery wing
to aid its dispersal.

Due to the ceaseless shifting
of its broken landscape the
Undercliff has suffered little disturbance
from man. – such a landscape does not invite
exploitation, and a succession of plant communities
has been free to develop without interference. In the chasm,
a climax of Ash wood is believed to be the largest example known of
its kind, having developed on virgin soil over the best part of
seventy years, completely undisturbed by man.

A large mouse scurrying up
a tree trunk? – no, it's a
treecreeper. Aptly named,
it feeds on tree trunks,
hitching itself up vertically
in a series of short spurts,
its tail pushing against
the bark.

   Having searched a tree, it
flits down to the base of the
next. The thin curved bill is
perfectly shaped to penetrate
cracks in the tree bark, pincering
out small insects
and larvae.

① egg laid singly
on bud stems,
hatches in
one week.
(also laid on
base of
caly x)
×10

② 4th instar, pupates
at 4-6 weeks
×2

③ first generation pupa
hatches in 2-3 weeks,
the second overwinters
hatching in March - April
×3

Holly Blue
(Celastrina argiolus)

♀ × 15

♀ × 3

Overwintering as a chrysalis it is the
earliest blue to emerge and the only butterfly
whose larval food plant changes from season to
season. The spring brood is normally found on holly, and
the summer generation on ivy, although in both cases other
plants such as gorse or spindle may occasionally be substituted.

Silver-washed Fritillary
(Argynnis paphia) ♀ x 3

At the edge of this clearing I see a butterfly
gliding down from the canopy. It floats
down onto a sunlit patch of grass where it
rests for a while.
    The wings fold showing the pale
silver-washed green of its underside that gives
the butterfly its name.

Ivy Broomrape
(Orobanche hederae)

Some parasitic plants
have a peculiar and unhealthy
appearance due to their lack
of chlorophyll, but the structure
and subtle reddish coloration
of the lesser broomrape render
it an attractive plant.

Along with wild clematis and ivy, honeysuckle is one of the plants that makes long lianas, which drape from and entangle the trees in Goat Island and other parts of the Undercliff. By August it is at the height of its flowering period. Each flower cluster consists of eight or more tubular flowers, each bearing nectar at the base. Many of the long-tongued insects feed on this.

The wren — surely the noisiest bird in the
Undercliff, even if it is one of the smallest! It feeds
mainly in the lower vegetation and undergrowth. Apparently,
wrens were almost wiped out in the harsh winter of 1962/3, but
they have certainly made a come-back since then.

The pigmy shrew (*Sorex minutus*)
is close to the minimum size at which a warm-blooded animal
can exist. If it were any smaller, its body surface would be so extensive
in relation to its bulk
that it would lose
heat too rapidly
to maintain a warm
body temperature.
As it is, the shrew must
work hard to replace the energy it

Woodlice are common
in the pigmy shrew's diet.

loses through body heat, but this entails
  using energy in the search for food … which must
    be replaced … and so it continues, the cycle following a three hourly
      pattern – 3 hours continuous feeding, 3 hours rest, 3 hours feeding.
      When the temperature drops, refuelling must be even more frequent. Without
      these constant meals, the shrew will die.

Sexton Beetle (Necrophorus vespillo)
working at a shrew corpse –
scrapes away soil beneath
it – corpse falls into
chamber. Female
remains in chamber,
makes ball of half
digested carrion. Grubs
first feed on this; when
larger, migrate to carcase.
Pupates in approx 2 weeks.

N. vespillo
has curved hind
tibia

A still June afternoon, hanging with a
dense warmth that makes me long
for thunder and the green smell that comes with lightning. Another twist in the
path, more creeper, another ridge to climb and here, unexpected, an opening, a

window in the dense foliage, admitting a current of cool air which I stand and enjoy as if it were a glass of iced water. Turning southwards to look out from this window, I am doubly refreshed – the sea – not, as I had expected, further ridges of dense vegetation but a steep scrub-covered slope ending in a litter of stone and boulders and – the sea.

Bright bird music coming from
high in the wood edge above the slope
— a superb song, as musical as a
blackbird's, low warbles rising to
rich liquid notes. It is a blackcap,
singing his boundaries. Summer visitors,
they are heard from April to early July, having
arrived at the end of March to stay
until early August

Rock-rose (*Helianthemum nummularium*)

The tissue-paper petals look slightly crumpled as if the
petals are not yet fully developed. A member of the same
family as the Mediterranean cistus, its Latin name
helianthemum means 'sun flower'

At various points along the footpath there look to be trails leading off to either side. For a long time I thought these were made by walkers foolishly ignoring the notices about the need to keep to the footpath; it was not until I was granted a permit to leave the path that I discovered their true origin. The first that I followed seemed a perfectly clear and logical trail for the first 50 metres or so – before it continued under a tangle of bramble in a gap far too low for humans to negotiate. Where the stems crossed

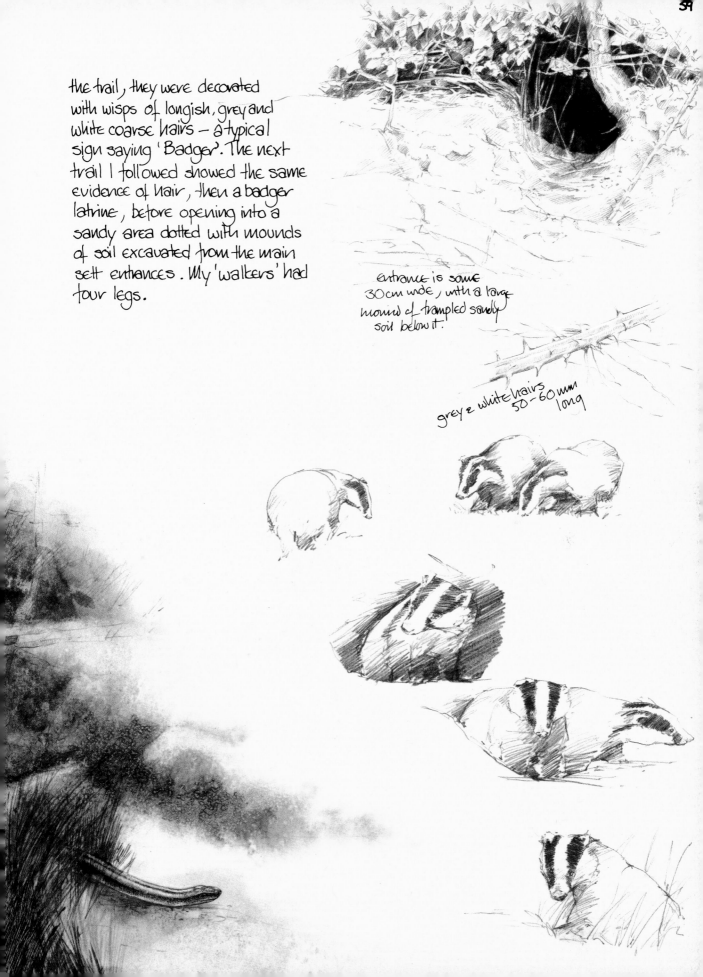

the trail, they were decorated with wisps of longish, grey and white coarse hairs – a typical sign saying 'Badger'. The next trail I followed showed the same evidence of hair, then a badger latrine, before opening into a sandy area dotted with mounds of soil excavated from the main sett entrances. My 'walkers' had four legs.

entrance is some 30 cm wide, with a large mound of trampled sandy soil below it.

grey & white hairs 50–60 mm long

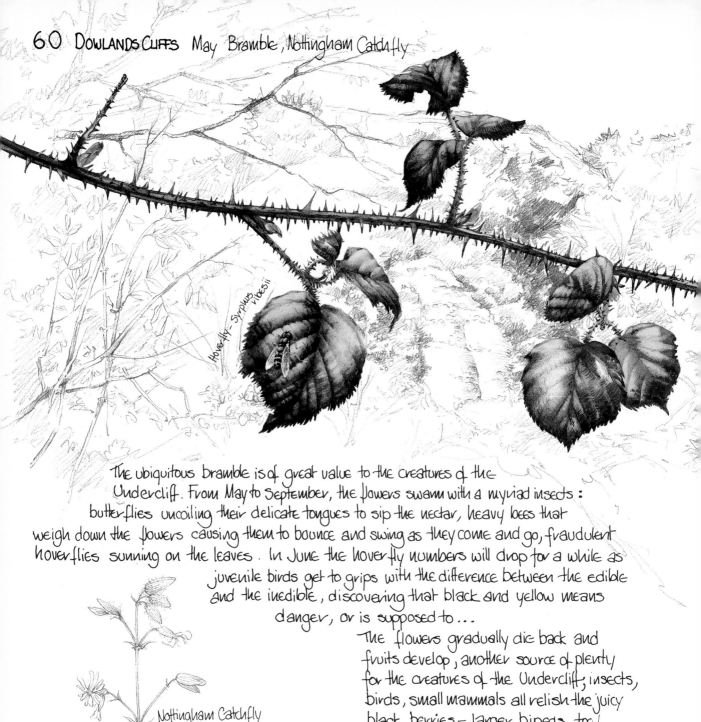

Hoverfly – Syrphus ribesii

Nottingham Catchfly
(Silene nutans)

The ubiquitous bramble is of great value to the creatures of the
Undercliff. From May to September, the flowers swarm with a myriad insects :
butterflies uncoiling their delicate tongues to sip the nectar, heavy bees that
weigh down the flowers causing them to bounce and swing as they come and go, fraudulent
hoverflies sunning on the leaves. In June the hoverfly numbers will drop for a while as
juvenile birds get to grips with the difference between the edible
and the inedible, discovering that black and yellow means
danger, or is supposed to...

The flowers gradually die back and
fruits develop, another source of plenty
for the creatures of the Undercliff; insects,
birds, small mammals all relish the juicy
black berries – larger bipeds, too!

Several rare plants find a haven in the Undercliff, including
Nottingham Catchfly. Being a plant of dry slopes, cliffs and
rocky debris, it has an ideal habitat here and, most important of
all, cannot be reached by plant hunters and trowels.
A night-flowering plant, it begins after dusk to
exhale a scent attractive to the moths that pollinate it.
The plant is not insectivorous but the top of the stems
are covered with sticky hairs, hence the name.

1.
Buds begin to
burst

2.

Not only does the bramble provide
a valuable food source . The tangled thickets
which it forms are superb nesting sites for a
variety of birds , including dunnocks, thrushes
blackbirds and finches .

3.
The petals die back and the
fruits begin to form .

4.
As they swell , the
colour develops from green through
light red to crimson, and finally
a glossy purple black.

When found in gardens, this caterpillar is a certain target for the 'if it moves, spray it' type of gardener, for it can defoliate soft fruit bushes. On examining it through a magnifying glass, I find I can forgive the damage it does to my evonymus for the sake of its bright colour and intricate pattern. Here in the Undercliff it causes little damage, the caterpillars feeding on spindle, hawthorn, sloe and pennywort.

Eggs are laid on the underside of leaves, hatching in ten days or so depending on the weather. The looper caterpillar hibernates over winter, emerging in May to resume feeding. By late June or early July, the black and yellow chrysalis will be formed, the imago emerging to fly throughout July and August.

caterpillar x 5.5

Magpie Moth
(Abraxas grossulariata)

♂ imago x 1

Cuckoo Pint (Arum maculatum) - also known as Lords and Ladies, Priests Pintle and Parson in the Pulpit.

First appears in April — a green sheath enclosing separate male and female flowers.

Gives off an odour that attracts small flies — these are trapped in the sheath by downward-pointing hairs and released when the sheath withers after pollination.

fruits have started to swell

sheath cut away to show internal structure.

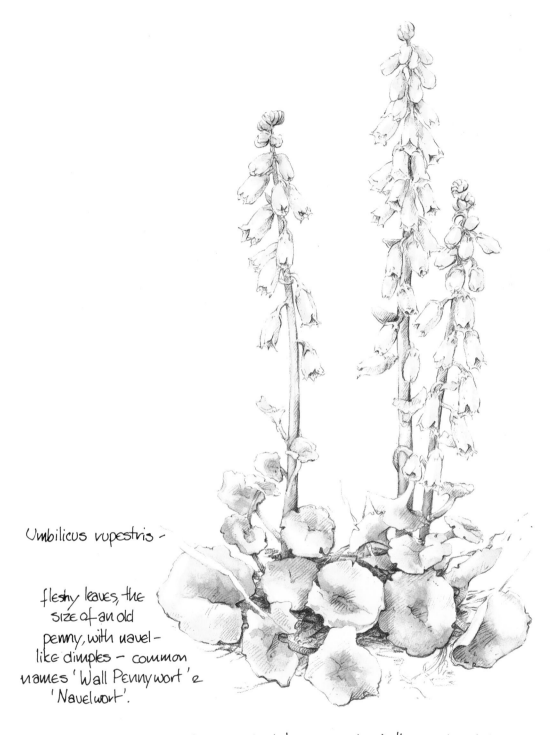

Umbilicus rupestris -

fleshy leaves, the
size of an old
penny, with navel-
like dimples - common
names 'Wall Pennywort' &
'Navelwort'.

Common plant found growing in the cracks of damp
rocks. At this time of the year, it carries long spikes of
tubular, greenish-cream flowers. The reddish stems may
grow up to 35 cm in length and, along with the leaves, will
wither after the seeds have ripened. The plant spends the
autumn and winter as an underground tuber.

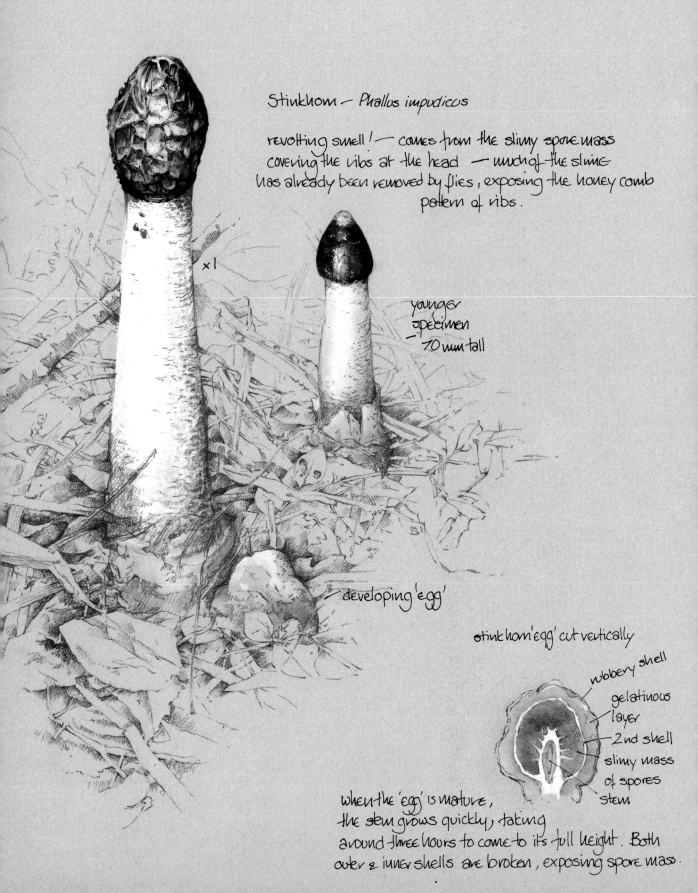

Stinkhorn — *Phallus impudicus*

revolting smell! — comes from the slimy spore mass
covering the ribs at the head — much of the slime
has already been removed by flies, exposing the honey comb
pattern of ribs.

×1

younger
specimen
— 70 mm tall

developing 'egg'

stinkhorn 'egg' cut vertically

rubbery shell
gelatinous
layer
2nd shell
slimy mass
of spores
stem

when the 'egg' is mature,
the stem grows quickly, taking
around three hours to come to its full height. Both
outer & inner shells are broken, exposing spore mass

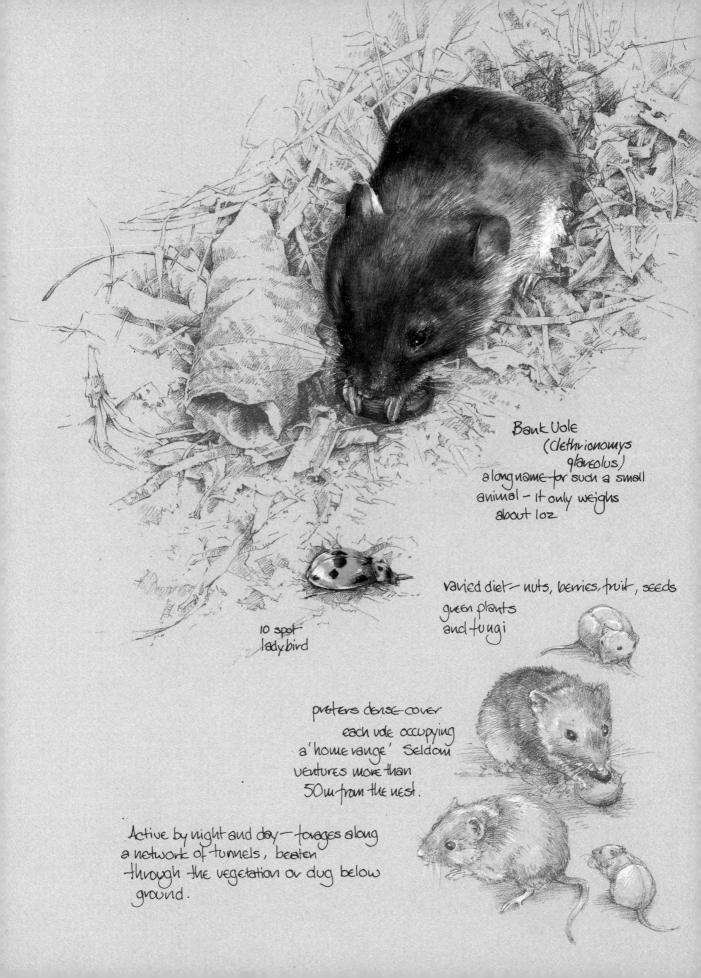

Bank Vole
(clethrionomys
glaveolus)
a long name for such a small
animal — it only weighs
about 1oz

varied diet — nuts, berries, fruit, seeds
green plants
and fungi

10 spot
ladybird

prefers dense cover
each vole occupying
a 'home range' Seldom
ventures more than
50m from the nest.

Active by night and day — forages along
a network of tunnels, beaten
through the vegetation or dug below
ground.

A screech - dark movement against the light -
a jay goes screaming away among the trees,
white rump patches catching the
shifting light filtered down through
the branches

wing feathers

Crest is
often raised
and lowered

Its short round wings
and long tail enable the
Jay to slip from
tree to tree in dense
cover. The bright blue
wing patches are most noticeable
when the bird is at rest or hopping
jerkily from branch
to branch.

Blue tit — an extrovert acrobat, the sprightly
Tom tit seems always on the move, never still.

Birch

Leaves beginning
to change colour —
yellowing from
edge inwards.

Some show
evidence of much
insect damage earlier
in the year. Birch supports some
229 insect species.

A Blue tit
will seldom win an argument
with a Great tit.

The Great tit supplements
its diet with eggs and
young birds.

Great tit ♂

The dominant member
of the tit family. Males have
brighter plumage than females —
underparts richer yellow, black
cap glossy not dull, black stripe
down middle is wider.

Hemp Nettle
(Galeopsis tetrahit) —
a particularly furry example

Perched on twig above my head, a belligerent robin displays its breast and lays claim to its territory in song. It will have paired some weeks ago in early January and will probably begin nest-building soon.

The Undercliff robins seem to have little fear of me as I walk along. On one occasion a particularly curious robin accompanied me for quite some distance, flitting from bush to bush and hopping along the path behind me. Perhaps it sensed that my lunch and sandwich crumbs were in the offing!

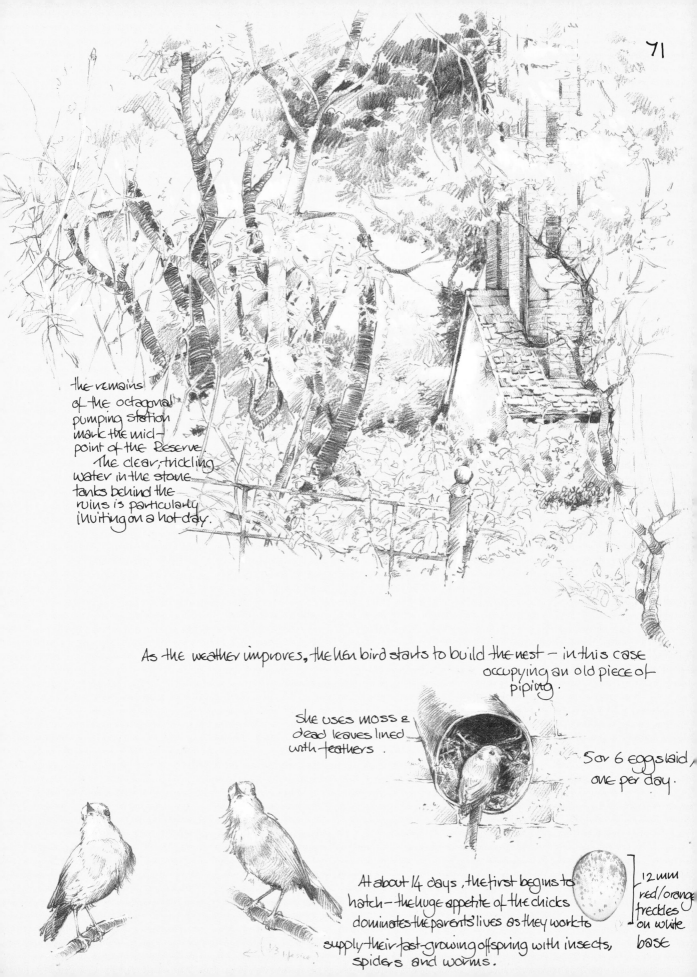

the remains
of the octagonal
pumping station
mark the mid-
point of the Reserve.
The clear, trickling
water in the stone
tanks behind the
ruins is particularly
inviting on a hot day.

As the weather improves, the hen bird starts to build the nest — in this case
occupying an old piece of
piping.

She uses moss &
dead leaves lined
with feathers.

5 or 6 eggs laid,
one per day.

At about 14 days, the first begins to
hatch — the huge appetite of the chicks
dominates the parents' lives as they work to
supply their fast-growing offspring with insects,
spiders and worms.

12mm
red/orange
freckles
on white
base

Japanese Knotweed (*Reynoutria japonica*)
   one of many exotics in the Undercliff. It may now be
considered a pernicious weed, but here its large
distinctive leaves are striking when seen against a
backdrop of ferns.

Scarlet Tiger
Moth
(Callimorpha × 1.5
dominula)

A quiet sun-baked shelf lower down
on the cliff — and this beautiful day-
flying moth appeared. Its flight had an
almost lazy pattern: it would seem to fall and
then pick itself up again at the last moment.

Looking over the slip near
Allhallows — the cliff slope is dotted
with large clumps of Pampas Grass.

× 1.5

The caterpillars feed in
groups on a variety of plants,
emerging from hibernation in April.

Spotted Flycatcher — not
really spotted at all, the
slightly darker streaks on
crown & breast are hardly
noticeable.

- A stove pipe stamped
'Burslem' - presumably,
imported from the
Potteries.

All that remains of
the range - one of its
door surrounds.

Situated south of the footpath, the ruins of
West Cliff Cottage stand as a reminder of earlier occupation of the Undercliff. Built by Ames in
1830, it marked the western extreme of the former Clevelands Estate (now Whitlands).
It is only over the last twenty years or so that the building has become so ruinous,
much of the decay having been assisted by people armed with metal detectors.
    At the eastern end of the estate, its partner appropriately named East Cliff Cottage has
fragmented even further as a result of land slipping. West Cliff Cottage appears to have been an early
single cell building which was given a new façade of expensive stonework at the time of its
re-development. The quality of both stone and brick suggests that some care was taken over its re-
building, the dressings being of Portland Stone. The windows have undergone some change during the life of
the cottage, for example the eastern most window of the second storey has been cut through the original
masonry, at a later date made to half size with hand blocked brick and stone rubble. Other windows
have three lintels. The earliest, of wood, presumably became soft through decay and was replaced by
one of a low grade stone, which in its turn was superceded by a new wooden one.

Three / four year old ♂
Beginning of white rings around eyes
and strip of fur between
eye and antler turning
white at top. Has not yet
developed suspicious
expression of an older animal.

A couple of people have remarked to me that roe like chocolate — perhaps I'm using the wrong brand — I generally seem to see their rear ends, moving fast — still, at least I can tell whether they are male or female!

Grey/brown ♂ winter pelage has white rump patch, becomes smaller and less distinct with summer coat.

The roe doe drops its fawns in June, usually in the dense undergrowth.

Spurge Laurel (Daphne Laureola) — neither a spurge nor a laurel.

Here, where there are no sheep, the hoof slots of roe are very distinctive — can often be seen crossing/following the footpath.

This track was down to the pumping station which
supplies the surrounding area with 400,000 gallons
of water a day.

Spring comes early to the Undercliff. Eager to benefit from the light available before the tree canopy leafs over, primroses hurry into flower. In the drizzle and downpour they are a glorious sign, a one-coloured rainbow promising that the rain will stop and we shall not drown in the winter dark.

On close inspection, the primrose shows two distinct types of flower centre:

1. Pin-eyed the style is elongated, the stigma appearing like a pin head at the top of the corolla tube. The stamens are attached lower down the tube.

2. Thrum-eyed - this arrangement has a short style with the stigma set below the stamens, which are at the top of the corolla tube. (A thrum is the fringe of threads left on the loom after the web is cut off + v.t. "to provide with a fringe".)

Initially this seems a peculiar variation, but it does make a great deal of sense. As the stigma of one flower type is in approximately the same position as the stamens of the other, cross pollination is ensured, resulting in strong plants.

Cowslips may be found in the more open areas of the Undercliff — generally they are plants of established calcareous grassland. The cowslip has long been used by man, notably to make a wine said to prevent madness, memory loss, headache and insomnia. The plant also has a history of being used in cosmetic preparations, though the word cowslip is of a more earthy derivation — from the Old English cu-slyppe (cow dung).

×1

Before long the daffodils will be in flower too.

Where cowslips and primrose are growing in close association, a few examples of the false oxlip (Primula veris x vulgaris) crop up. The flowers are similar to those of the primrose but are held, cowslip-like, in a group at the top of a long stalk.

7.00 Dusk after a clear evening, promising frost. Nearby but unseen, a pair of owls call and answer "kerwic" – "to-whoo" – Tawnies here also call at midday – often quite promptly.

Seldom seen, but often heard, Tawny Owls hold small hunting territories throughout the Undercliff, the same perches being used regularly. Wood mice are their chief food here.

Another night caller frequents the woodland. Often arriving with the blackthorn flowers, the Nightingale reaches the Undercliff in mid-April and singing males are often heard from late April through to early June.

The Long-tailed Tit must benefit from the shelter of the Undercliff — a delicate bird, particularly susceptible to the effects of bad weather. Its behaviour is similar to that of other members of the tit family - active and restless, always searching twigs and branches for insects. The rounded body and long tail give it a top-heavy look in the air. The flight has an undulating pattern.

In winter the tits flock together in groups of up to 20 — in flight they don't bunch together but flit from tree to tree in ones and twos, always maintaining contact with a low trill or si-si-si , similar to other titmice

often land on twigs upside down

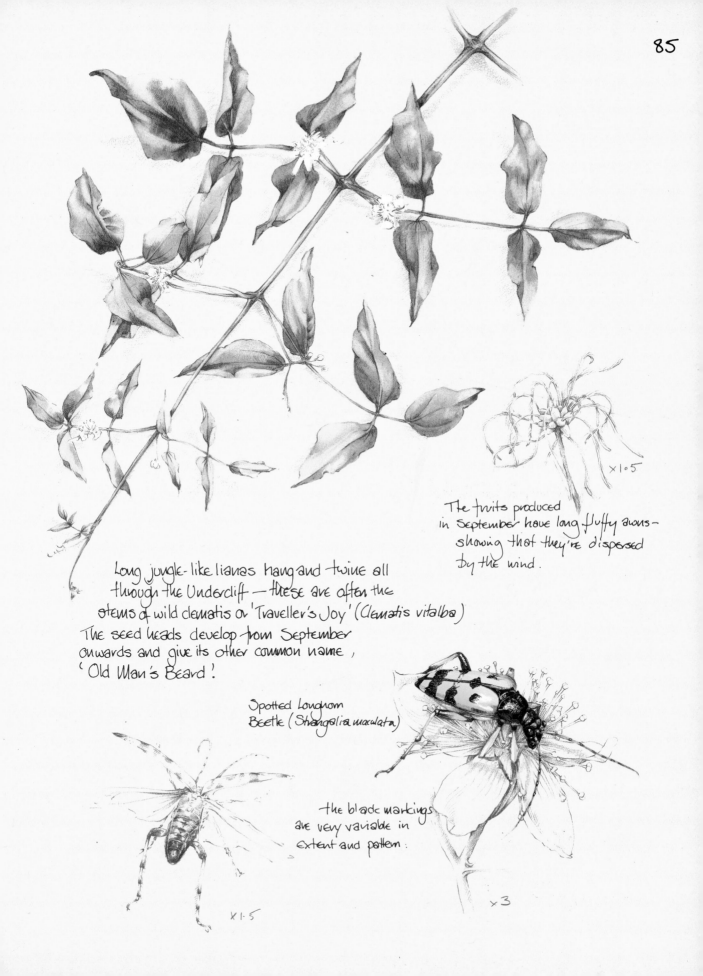

×1·5

The fruits produced
in September have long fluffy awns—
showing that they're dispersed
by the wind.

Long jungle-like lianas hang and twine all
through the Undercliff — these are often the
stems of wild clematis or 'Traveller's Joy' (Clematis vitalba)
The seed heads develop from September
onwards and give its other common name,
'Old Man's Beard'.

Spotted Longhorn
Beetle (Strangalia maculata)

the black markings
are very variable in
extent and pattern.

×1·5

×3

A favourite haunt of mallard, this system of ponds
was cleared in 1984. I feel it a privilege to stand
here, for although the deer come here to drink,
it isn't an easy place for humans to find – getting
here involved at least an hour of scrambling through
undergrowth that at times seemed almost
impenetrable. The effort was well rewarded:
this still space of water is encircled by a tapestry
of vegetation – every shade of autumn is here,
all blended by a haze of drifting moisture,
half mist, half rain.

Wherever I look there is a new
play of colour – bracken, yellow bramble,
gold and green sedges, deep glass-green
water – but again and again I return
to the same place – a red gold
turkey oak against the
profound green of a holm.

88 PINHAY August Dormouse

Summer nest made in bushes etc, above
ground. Winter nest built on or below ground
level - eg. between tree roots. Some materials
used for both.

←15cm→

Basic requirements for dormouse life:
1. A good layer of shrubby undergrowth for food and protection with abundant growth of hazel.
2. Honeysuckle – its bark is stripped for nest building.
3. Peace, disturbed only by the dormouse's natural predators – owls, corvids and foxes.

Approx. 4ft above ground

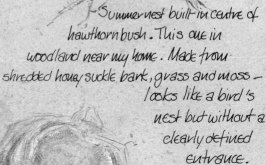

Summer nest built in centre of hawthorn bush. This one in woodland near my home. Made from shredded honeysuckle bark, grass and moss – looks like a bird's nest but without a clearly defined entrance.

Two litters a year of 3-4 young, leaving the nest at 30 days, sexually mature the following year.

Early Autumn – feasts on nuts and berries rapidly increasing fat reserves in preparation for hibernation

Our only truly hibernating mammals, dormice are now becoming rare. Hibernation starts September/October when the temperature drops below 15°C, and continues until some time in April, the dormouse waking briefly every few weeks.

The well stuffed dormouse – pot bellied and nearly spherical!

Rarely seen, the dormouse is strictly nocturnal and spends most of its waking time above ground, feeding in trees and bushes.

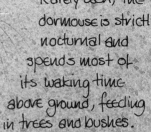

Note the large eyes, typical of a nocturnal mammal.

Feeds mainly on nuts, fruit and seeds, also pollen – occasionally takes insects.

Selfheal (Prunella vulgaris)
Overlooked or despised as a garden weed,
selfheal is a handsome plant, if
not a showy one.

Blue-purple flowers
from June to
October

Called selfheal from its former
use as a wound herb, early
 herbalists named it Prunella,
as it was also reputed to
cure sore throats,
then known by
that name.

Square stem,
evergreen leaves

×2

Grows in clumps, spreading
by short runners

Arion ater ×2

The name 'blackbird'
brings several ideas to mind:
two visual — the
graceful plié of
its tail
after landing,
the graphic black
and yellow of the male's
contrasting plumage, bill
and eyering;

and two aural —
its glorious
voice enriching the
bird chorus on a still
morning — and, less
lyrical, the hysterical and
explosive screech of alarm as it
dashes away if startled.

Some of the most common
birds in the Undercliff, they
are often seen kicking up the
leaf litter in search
of food.

Buddleja davidii

Buddleja thrives in the Undercliff,
a magnet for the resident
insect life.

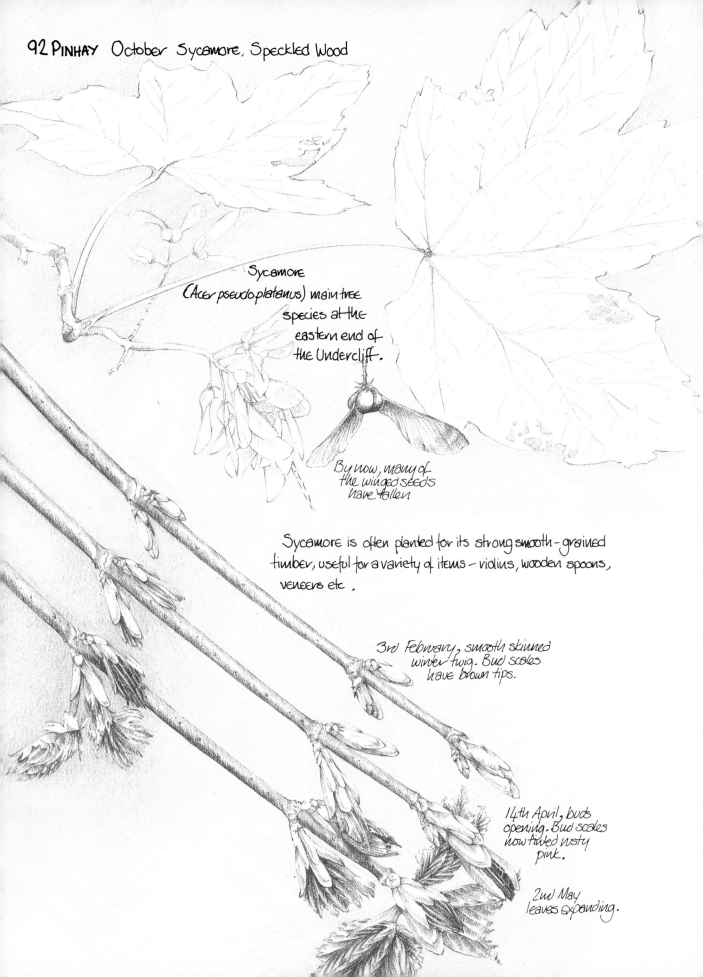

Sycamore
(Acer pseudo platanus) main tree
species at the
eastern end of
the Undercliff.

By now, many of
the winged seeds
have fallen

Sycamore is often planted for its strong smooth-grained
timber, useful for a variety of items – violins, wooden spoons,
veneers etc.

3rd February, smooth skinned
winter twig. Bud scales
have brown tips.

14th April, buds
opening. Bud scales
now tinted rusty
pink.

2nd May
leaves expanding.

Wood Sage.
(Teucrium scorodonia)
— nearly finished flowering

Newly emerged speckled
wood, in pristine condition,
resting in dappled shade.

Speckled Wood
(Pararge aegeria)
♀ x 1.5
Often seen in and
around the Undercliff,
generally in dappled or
light shade and I
get the impression
that it has increased
in numbers over
the last few
years.

0.8mm

1. Yellow/white
egg laid singly on grass blade,
hatches after approx. 10 days,
eating shell.

2. Newly hatched caterpillar -
feeds on grasses. First instar
has shiny black head
and cream body.

2.5mm

3. Fully grown caterpillar,
4 weeks after hatching
(or seven months if overwintering
as larva) 2nd & 3rd instars
have green head and
body with darker
green lines.

27mm

4. Pupa, attached to a
pad of silk on a grass
stem. Colour is
variable — light/dark,
brownish/green. Hatches
after 3-4 weeks or over winters,
hatching mid to late March

12.5mm

Two kinds of oak can be seen in the Undercliff, the Turkey Oak (Quercus cerris) and the evergreen Holm Oak (Quercus ilex). As its name suggests, the leaves from basal shoots and saplings of the latter look very much like holly leaves — decidedly prickly. Leaves on higher branches lose their prickly character, becoming smooth edged — also like holly.

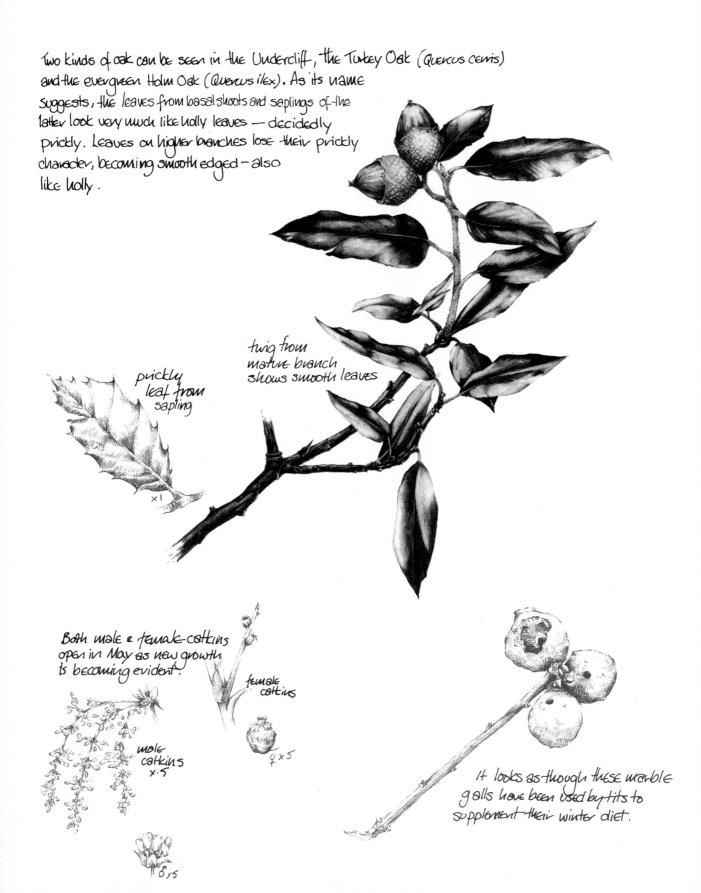

twig from mature branch shows smooth leaves

prickly leaf from sapling

×1

Both male & female catkins open in May as new growth is becoming evident.

female catkins

male catkins ×·5

♀ ×5

♂ ×5

It looks as though these marble galls have been used by tits to supplement their winter diet.

Corpse of a song thrush—
from it I can see that
the characteristic
breast spots are
formed by dark brown
barbs at the tips of some
of the breast feathers.

Thrushes are usually
solitary, but sometimes
roost in winter with visiting
redwings and fieldfares — these
feed in flocks on the cliff-top during
cold winter months.

A thrush has clearly been smashing
open snail shells on this stone 'anvil.'
There are remains of both Cepaea hortensis
& Cepaea nemoralis, the white & dark
lipped banded snails.

Thrushes apparently use
resonance to test for empty shells —
these can often be found around anvils

The 'descending terraces of Pinhay' (once known as Pinney) are constantly on the move, new cracks and fissures always opening up along the sides of the footpath.

In 1966 the path down to the shore was destroyed by a slip which also broke the water-supply to the house above. A great flow of mud poured over the cliffs taking many trees with it; large numbers were completely uprooted and destroyed, but others survived the gradual slide towards the sea and have re-rooted at a variety of angles.

Unmolested by hunting or poisoning, foxes must have a peaceful time here. Although their numbers dropped dramatically because of the myxomatosis epidemic in the 1950s, they are now abundant once again. Foxes are mainly nocturnal, but they can be seen above ground during the day, particularly in summer when they often spend daylight hours resting up in dense undergrowth.

fox
skull
x .5

As a child I remember imagining all kinds of frightful happenings when I heard the gasping scream that I now know to be a vixen calling. It can still raise a shiver when I hear it on a quiet winter's night. I have never heard either vixen or dog-fox (a dry coughing bark) call in bad weather — they seem to dislike the wind and wet.

At last spring is fully underway, even hints that summer
is not too far off. Several of the smaller flowering plants
are taking advantage of the light available before the
leaf cover becomes dense, and are well into their
flowering periods.

An introduced alien, the periwinkle
spreads as the leaf nodes of a
recumbent stem root and form a
new plant. According to Culpeper,
'the young tops made into a
consewe is good for the
nightmare' — curing or giving?

Greater Periwinkle (Vinca major)
lifesize

It's impossible to capture this kind of blue with pigment.

flowers have straight, un-notched spurs.

Pale Wood Violet (*Viola reichenbachiana*) ×1·25

This particular plant had flowers of a striking electric blue rather than the more usual lilac. I presume this to be the result of the extremely chalky soil it was growing on.

The Underdliff is rich with ferns
and mosses - soft shield fern, broad buckler,
great banks of hartstongue thrive on the
calcareous soil. Here, feathered stands of
male fern arch up between tree roots.
Nourished by the decay of lush
vegetation, they grow to a great
size in the warm, moist air of
the woodland.

An outraged Devils
Coach Horse
(Staphylinus olens)

Male Fern
(Dryopteris filix-mas) ×1

Hartstongue
(Phyllitis scolopendrium) ×1

fronds are solid and
strangely unfernlike.

Underside of Male Fern
frond × 1 —
up to 12 sori
on each lobe.

Painted Lady - *Vanessa cardui*

Thick
legged Flower
Beetle ×1
*Oedemera
nobilis* —
only the male has
the thickened
hind legs

neat rounded
sections missing
from leaf edges —
a sure sign that
leaf-cutter bees
are at work

Dog Rose (*Rosa canina*) ×1 — flowers vary
from pink to white, found in many places
throughout the Underliff, flowering late May
to July. The root stock of this rose used for
grafting hybrid garden roses.

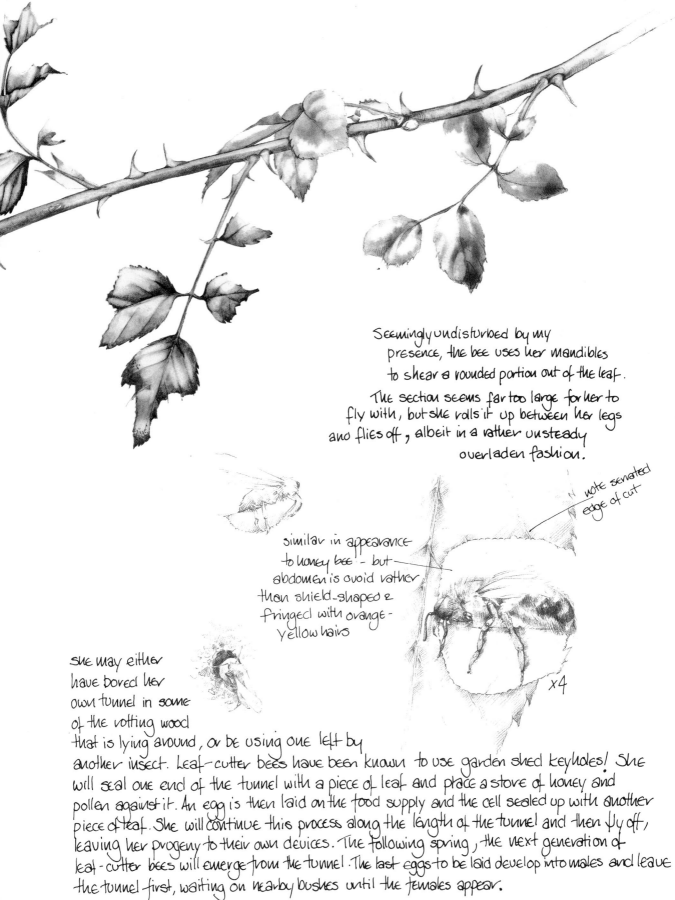

Seemingly undisturbed by my
presence, the bee uses her mandibles
to shear a rounded portion out of the leaf.

The section seems far too large for her to
fly with, but she rolls it up between her legs
and flies off, albeit in a rather unsteady
overladen fashion.

note serrated
edge of cut

similar in appearance
to honey bee — but
abdomen is ovoid rather
than shield-shaped &
fringed with orange-
yellow hairs

×4

She may either
have bored her
own tunnel in some
of the rotting wood
that is lying around, or be using one left by
another insect. Leaf-cutter bees have been known to use garden shed keyholes! She
will seal one end of the tunnel with a piece of leaf and place a store of honey and
pollen against it. An egg is then laid on the food supply and the cell sealed up with another
piece of leaf. She will continue this process along the length of the tunnel and then fly off,
leaving her progeny to their own devices. The following spring, the next generation of
leaf-cutter bees will emerge from the tunnel. The last eggs to be laid develop into males and leave
the tunnel first, waiting on nearby bushes until the females appear.

A flash of blue-grey across the path, I
look to follow the bird through my
binoculars but it is gone, leaving merely an
impression of colour and movement
against a column of sunlight.

Note the bill — stout enough to
hammer open nuts, but also
slender enough to probe for
insects & spiders

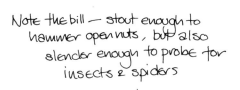

x2

Much of the nuthatch's diet is made up of
such items as nuts, beechmast and acorns
which it wedges into a crevice in tree bark,
hammering away with its stout woodpecker-like
bill to split the nut and extract the kernel.

A harsh laughing call is often the
only evidence that there is a Green Woodpecker nearby, for they are
shy birds and will slip away at the approach of a human. Their flight is markedly undulating,
as if they were bounding along a path of invisible springboards. On the down-glide, the
wings are held close to the body, then the bird pulls upward with a few strong beats.
Attaining height, it ships oars to glide again.
The sharply pointed bill is well designed for
chiselling into bark in the hunt for wood-boring
insects, but the bird as often feeds
on the ground, excavating
ants' nests for the feasts
therein.

On the ground it has an upright,
alert jizz, hopping clumsily for
short distances.

The green coloration of the woodpecker's plumage is not produced by a pigment but by the structure of its feather barbs. These reflect only green light, the remainder of the spectrum passing through the barb to be absorbed by a dark layer of melanin. Together with the amount of feather dust a bird produces, the angle at which these barbs are set determines the lustre or dullness of its plumage.

barb
interlocked barbules

Shortly after sunset — over my head, a squeaking, darker
shadow skimming across patches of paynes grey sky — monochrome trees.
Britain's largest bat Nyctalus noctula starts to hunt. Flying high it
dives onto large insects, eating them in the air.

How could anyone dislike him
or think he belongs in a horror film?

Earlier in the day, at
the base of a fallen tree
I found a beautiful green
variety of 10 spot ladybird.

Adalia 10 punctata
x5

Noctule Bat (*Nyctalus noctula*) x 1·25
Primarily a woodland species, it has a
wingspan of up to 39 cm. Other bats
recorded in suitable areas of the reserve —
Pipistrelles, Long Eared and Lesser Horseshoe

Snowberry
Symphoricarpos
rivularis x·5

Spindle Tree
(Euonymus europaeus)
the berries of the
spindle are relished by
many birds in the Undercliff.
Spindle timber is very hard
and doesn't splinter – must have
proved useful to the cottagers who
once lived in the Undercliff.
Traditionally used for
making such items as
skewers and ... spindles.
Also produces excellent charcoal.

Unlike the red, which is a
cone and shoot eater,
the grey squirrel seems to
prefer feeding on the ground, especially
in the autumn when hazel nuts and acorns
fall to the ground, either naturally or when foraging squirrels
shake the branches. It
spends
25% of its time
up in the trees.

Food is fairly
varied - the expected acorns, beech mast,
hazels etc, plus berries, crab
apples, leaf buds, some
types of bark and a
few of the available
fungi

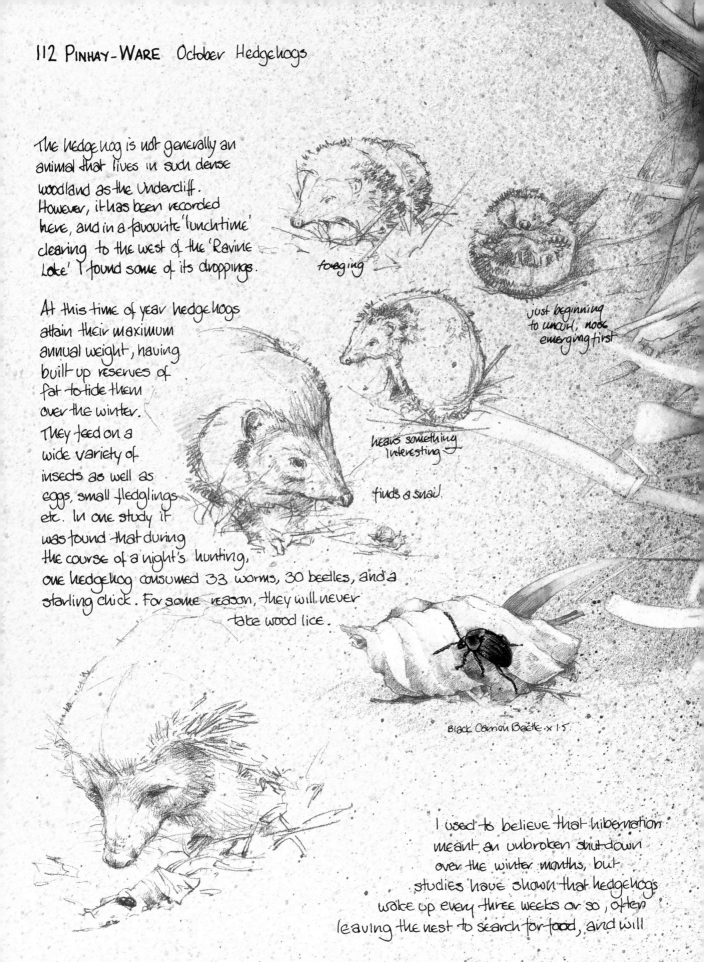

The hedgehog is not generally an animal that lives in such dense woodland as the Undercliff. However, it has been recorded here, and in a favourite 'lunchtime' clearing to the west of the 'Ravine Lake' I found some of its droppings.

At this time of year hedgehogs attain their maximum annual weight, having built up reserves of fat to tide them over the winter. They feed on a wide variety of insects as well as eggs, small fledglings etc. In one study it was found that during the course of a night's hunting, one hedgehog consumed 33 worms, 30 beetles, and a starling chick. For some reason, they will never take wood lice.

foraging

just beginning to uncurl, nose emerging first

hears something interesting

finds a snail.

Black Carrion Beetle x 1.5

I used to believe that hibernation meant an unbroken shutdown over the winter months, but studies have shown that hedgehogs wake up every three weeks or so, often leaving the nest to search for food, and will

even change their nest site during the course of
the winter. The nest, or hibernaculum, is made of
tightly packed leaves which form an insulating layer,
keeping the interior, complete with snoring hedgepig,
at an optimum hibernating temperature.

These goldfinches are only
partial migrants; the group - or
'charm' may be leaving shortly to overwinter
down the western side of Europe; or perhaps they will take advantage of the shelter
and food supply provided by the Undercliff to overwinter here.

They are adept at using their feet to aid feeding. A little earlier in the year, I
observed one holding a sow-thistle seed head against
its perch with one foot as it picked out the seed.

Unlike many other
birds, goldfinches
don't have a
spring moult
into breeding
plumage

The bright
colours emerge as the dull
feather tips wear away.

Goldfinches always seem to
be illustrated feeding from teasel heads, but they take seeds from a wide range of
compositae — thistles, dandelions, ragwort etc. The sharply pointed bill enables the
bird to get down to the seeds past the silky hairs that allow these seeds to be
distributed by the wind. Judging from several
preserved skins it seems that the male
generally has a slightly larger bill than
a female of comparable size.

X 1

The Ravine Lake —

a long still-surfaced pool — always a
favourite stopping place. It's worth braving the midges
for the dragonflies and damselflies which
come here to hunt, mate and lay eggs.

Aeshna cyanea x1·25

The life cycle is a comparatively long one for an insect — about a year from egg to adult damselfly, but often two or three years for the dragonfly.

Mating is a curious procedure. Sperm is transferred from the male's genitals, which are in the last but one segment of his body, to special mating organs in the second segment. He grasps the female at the back of the head with pincers on his tail and she bends her body round so that her tail end comes into contact with the mating organs.

The nymphs are surprisingly ugly — the dragonflies rather drab in colour, the damselflies varying from bright green to dull brown — and have voracious appetites. They live and feed among the water weed and mud at the bottom of the pond and have an intriguing adaptation to the lower lip to enable them to catch prey.

This 'mask', a hinged structure, has pincer-like extensions which shoot out to catch the prey.

Ischnura elegans mating
× 2.5

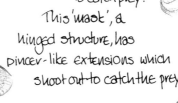

mask shooting out to catch tadpole

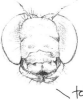

folded mask

Marsh Tit (Parus palestris)
Generally very difficult to distinguish
marsh from willow tit — up to the
beginning of this century, they
were thought to be the same
species. The willow tit
prefers wetter ground,
it's call a nasal 'tchair'. Usually the willow has pale wing
panels and a glossy
crown, although these
are only evident given
unusually good
visibility.

dull crown

smooth
plumage

The Undercliff is home to
marsh tits — despite its
name this tit is not a
marshland bird, preferring
damp woodland or hedgerows
where it frequents the lower growth.
Scurrying in the undergrowth it can be
difficult to see and is often more
readily located by ear — call is
'pitchew - pitchew'.

Bloody Nosed Beetle (Timarcha tenebricosa) —
has a curious method of defence if molested, exudes a
drop of bright red fluid from mouth — a mixture of
blood and bitter tasting chemical deterrent. May
also feign death if
attack continues.

Bloody nosed beetle
× 2·5

wing cases
fused together

very long tibia
and broad tarsi

flower structure
× 1.5

Bugle (Ajuga reptans) × 1.5
flower is a beautiful misty blue and intricately
shaped. Hybrid forms now often grown in gardens.

For elegance of line, the
arching flower stems of Carex pendula
can hardly be bettered. It occurs
throughout the damp areas of the
Undercliff, and here at Ware,
grows in abundance.

Ware also provides suitable
habitat for the grass snake
and the toad.

Natrix natrix helvetica and   Bufo bufo
- most predators are deterred by the poison
glands on the toad's back, but grass snakes
will sometimes take them.

Pendulous Sedge (Carex pendula)

June 2nd, about 10·20 a.m. , female smooth newt laying eggs,
moves around several plants, grasps a leaf with her hind legs, drops
a single egg on it and folds the leaf around the egg, still using
her hind feet.

five toes & four
fingers

During the breeding
season, the tail spine
of the male may be
up to
10mm long

Palmate ♂ x 1·5 May
Note black webs on hind feet
indicating breeding season

Dytiscus marginalis larva
x2

x2

One of the many predators of newt tadpoles is the
Great Diving Beetle (*Dytiscus marginalis*). The large
larvae are particularly ferocious and will attack and eat
virtually anything they can catch. They feed by injecting
digestive juices into the prey and
sucking out the pre-digested
body fluids.

The undisturbed ponds and wetter areas of the Undercliff provide a good habitat for newts. Smooth, palmate and great crested newts have all been recorded here. The latter is very rare, and I have as yet seen only the first two.

Great Diving Beetle
(Dytiscus marginalis)

Smooth Newt ♂

Smooth Newt ♀

The lush vegetation and many ponds of this area make it ideal for frogs.

20th March egg swells and rises to surface

28th March development visible

tadpoles hatching around 9th April

these sketches were made from tadpoles developing in my own garden pond.

back legs appear 8th May

amplexus observed 18th March

all legs developed 30th May

tail still present but quickly goes

leaves pond 2nd June.

the hind feet have webs of skin between the toes, connecting them for about ½ their length. These enable the frog to move efficiently in water.

The frog preys on a variety of smaller creatures. It catches insects with a flick of the tongue, munches snails complete with shell, and is the best slug assassin a gardener could wish for. It enjoys earthworms too, and, preferring a clean meal to one covered in earth, the frog will scrape off the dirt with its front feet as it swallows the unfortunate worm.

Long hind legs enable the frog to get out of trouble — if it can see the trouble coming.

An average adult some 75 mm in length can clear up to half a metre in one leap.

Mature ♀ × 1.5

It is early July and the exodus of froglets is almost at an end. Many have been ready to leave the pond for some time, but the weather has been dry and they have stayed at the margin, half submerged in the water that has been their home since they were spawned. Today the weather has broken; a brief monsoon makes the land more familiar and it is time for them to leave. Each is now a perfect but minute frog, an 'N' gauge amphibian, barely 13mm / ½ in. in length. A multitude of dangers awaits them: grass snakes, birds, rats, other amphibians. The frog must reproduce in phenomenal numbers to survive predators. Each female lays between 1,000 and 2,500 eggs. Of those that hatch, few tadpoles survive to leave the pond as they are a major food supply for its other inhabitants.

It's a tough life being a frog.

4.00 p.m. Pair of magpies on stile just
west of Underhill farm. Bold plumage
contrasted against the mid-green of
a dull afternoon.
   Startled, they fly off south westwards,
flight is unhurried, skimming low
over the scrub, dragging their
long tails over bushes.

A catholic diet — Insects, small
mammals and birds, worms and
other invertebrates. In spring they
take fledglings and eggs; in winter
grain, berries and other fruit

The Undercliff contains many plants that have been used in former times for medicinal purposes.

Note the 'keel' of fur along tail, and furry hind feet

Great Horsetail
(Equisetum telmateia)

Horsetails are common in the Undercliff, contributing to the exotic look of the place. Culpeper claims 'it solders together the tops of green wounds'. The plant was also used to polish silver because of the silica it contains.

sterile stem

spore carrying stem

Comfrey
(Symphytum officinale)

The flower of this old medicinal plant varies from white to mauve. It may have been grown by the cottagers for its welding properties— 'it is special good for ruptures and broken bones, yea it is said to be so powerful to consolidate and knit together that if it be boiled with dissevered pieces of flesh in a pot, it will join them together again'. The plant is still used medicinally for the allantoin extracted from its roots.

The raceme of bell-shaped flowers slowly uncurls, each flower paling as it ages.

Wood Avens or
Herb Bennet
(Geum urbanum)

A very common plant in the damp parts of the Undercliff.

Used as a febrifuge in acute and intermittent fevers since the Middle Ages.

Except when mating, no shrew will tolerate
another's presence in its territory.

All three species of shrew are well recorded in the Undercliff, including the least abundant —
the water shrew (*Neomys fodiens*) which normally prefers slow moving streams and is
very local throughout the country.

The beauty of apple blossom invites the
use of exhausted and sentimental clichés, but
only a hardened cynic could fail to be moved by it.
 Here in the lane it is a reminder of the
bungalow named the 'Orchard' which once stood
here, but had to be demolished in 1969 due to
the damage caused by land slipping in
this and the preceding year

Comma
(Polygonia c-album)
rather battered
looking

In the centre of the hind wing
(underside) is the comma-shaped
mark which gives the
English
name

In autumn, a new generation of commas
may come to the same tree to enjoy the
over-ripe windfalls.

1. March 15th, buds beginning
to burst on winter twig.

2. April 17th,
small pink
buds showing

Small Tortoiseshell (*Aglais urtica*), also worn.

Both this and the comma will be individuals from the generation that overwintered in hibernation.

3. May 4th, in full bloom

4. June 15th, fruitlets developing

132 WARE LANE   June   Foxglove, Spider, Cranefly

Although the soil is for the main
part strongly calcareous there
are areas where the calcifugous
foxglove finds a niche – it's
always a surprise to see it
amongst the wide array
of chalk-loving
species.

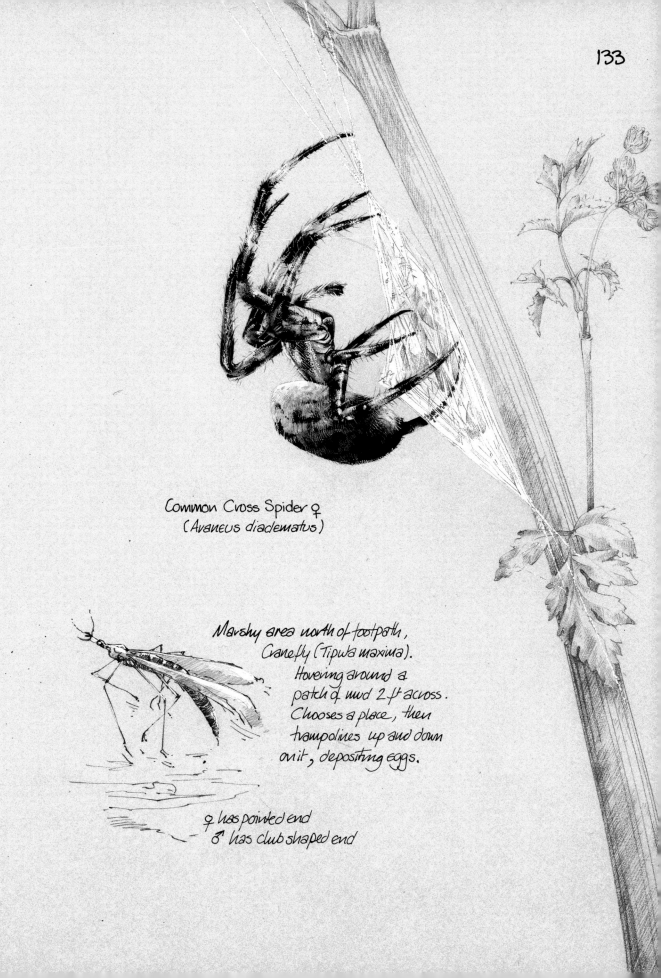

Common Cross Spider ♀
(Araneus diadematus)

Marshy area north of footpath,
Cranefly (Tipula maxima).
Hovering around a
patch of mud 2 ft across.
Chooses a place, then
trampolines up and down
on it, depositing eggs.

♀ has pointed end
♂ has club shaped end

Generally a butterfly of chalk grassland, the marbled white
   (*Melanargia galathea*) occurs in great numbers on the open
      slopes at Ware.
         The name has undergone some interesting changes
            over the last two hundred years. In the early 19th
         century the marbled white was known as the half-mourner,
      from the half way stage of mourning when a woman
   would change from black to black and white clothing.
      Some time later, the butterfly became known as the marmoress,
   from marmoreal, the adjective of 'marble'. Later in the 19th
century the butterfly became known by its present name.

flight
is slow
and lazy ♀

↕ 1mm   smooth white egg, round
   with flattened base. During
   July and August, eggs scattered
   at random, often while female is in
   flight. Hatches in approx. 3 weeks.

② ← 2·5 mm →   newly hatched larva, eats
   shell on emergence. Soon hibernates,
   overwintering as larva. Emerges to
   begin feeding in January or February.

fully grown larva
(4th instar)

← 28mm →

③

④ ← 14 mm   Pupates June/July on
   ground beneath grass.
   Seems to shrivel over
   4-5 days, then pupates,
   hatching in approx.
   three weeks.

cream/white

Harvestman.
(Phalangium
opilio)
has pure white
underside; ♂
has horned
chelicerae.

rubbery when fresh.

dries to a
horny,
leathery, texture

Ear Fungus (Auricularia auricula) –
found all year round, usually
on elder branches.
(this example found early May)

Standing in Devon, looking at Dorset — the gate marks
the county boundary — map ref: SY 29/39 331(.25) /916(.5).
    Just the other side of the hedge,
there is a large warren of very
prosperous looking rabbits. On   Sloping fields now fenced
this spring evening, a large   off for grazing
reddish buck and three sleek
does are quietly feeding, seeming not
to care that I am watching them.

Orange Tip (*Anthocharis cardamines*)

When the egg is first laid, it's a pale translucent green, but over the first day or so it changes to a deep orange colour, hatching after a week into a pale orange larva with a shiny black head.

x10

By the second instar, the body has become more green in colour and has developed a white lateral line

x10

♂ x 1·25

Garlic Mustard (*Alliaria petiolata*) also known as 'Jack by the Hedge' – a common plant, but handsome. Useful too – the leaves can be used in salads or steamed. Before garlic became a common ingredient, a sauce for salted fish was made from the flower heads. The mustard oil contained in its leaves was also used in medicinal preparations.

At the fourth and final instar, the head and body are bluish green shading to white on the sides and dark green on the ventral surface

x2

It would seem that for some reason the larvae never pupate on the food species, but always choose to attach themselves to another plant. The butterfly overwinters as a pupa; it will not emerge before the following spring.

x2

Lady's Smock.

(cardamine pratensis) Another of those
plants that show that spring is undeniably upon
us, with the promise of summer yet to come. It
comes into flower roughly when the cuckoo
starts to call in April and is gone in June, when
the cuckoo 'changes his tune'. The flowers are
a delicately shaded lilac pink, or occasionally white, and the formation of the
bloom shows it to be a member of
the cabbage family (Cruciferae)

♀

♂

The Mouldiwarp,
Moldewarp or
Earthkrower —
that is to say, mole —
leaves signs of his activities
all through the slip, even in areas
where the ground would seem unsuitably rocky.
No such problems at this end of the slip, however;
the light soil must make for easy tunnelling. Farther to the west,
under the tree cover at the side of Ware Lane, the mole heaves are instantly visible —
neat mounds of pale sandy soil contrasting with the dark leaf mould onto which they have been
cast up. On the footpath one sometimes comes across small holes 40-50 mm across where they have burrowed down to make a
permanent 'road'. From this they tunnel along side spurs, at the end of which are thrown up the familiar spoil heaps.

Moles have an extremely high metabolic rate, needing to eat around
half their body weight (100-130 gm) of
worms and other insects daily.
Unable to sit up on its haunches
to feed, the mole lowers
itself to the ground,
holding the prey
against the
ground with its front feet. The food is then torn apart
by upward jerks of the mole's head and swallowed rapidly. — No thoughtful
chewing for the mole!
Despite the fantasies of some authors, the mole is a
solitary and aggressive creature which will chase
away others that trespass into its territory. (A truce
is called during the brief mating season.)

sharp
teeth!

Walking up to the slip one bright morning I was surprised to come accross a dead mole in the middle of the path. There was no evidence of any injury to the animal which looked to be in good condition. The cause of death remained a mystery.

The moles' vertical fur enables easy movement in small tunnels.

Note the coat lacks the silvery sheen of the live animal. This disappears soon after death.

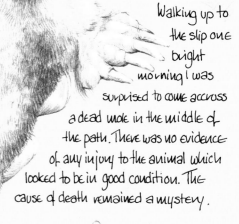

The claws are worn from digging, but show translucent tips.

molars premolars canine incisors

The large tooth in the lower jaw corresponds to the upper canine but is actually an elongated pre-molar.

Live moles carry their tails very upright, the small whiskers on the tail are very sensitive.

Safe here from ploughing and poisoning, the moles' main predators are badgers, which will take them, despite the moles' skin glands which, some say, make them distasteful to carnivores.

a brown, sparrow-sized
bird, like a small, slender
thrush — Rock pipit.

Although the nearest heronry is some distance
away, herons are occasionally seen flying along
the shoreline, presumably in search of eels.

A rock pipit bobs around the strandline, picking
up insects and bits of debris from the incoming tide.
It doesn't fly off until I am within eight feet of it.
   Examining the site where it was feeding, I see several
wood-louse like creatures - sea slaters

I had 'boulder-hopped' along the foreshore from Lyme to just below the pumping station; a gusting wind had blown rain and salt spray at me all the way. The raw end of a land slip is always fascinating, but on a dismal day in February this seemed more a statement of faith than of fact.

Shelduck can often
be seen on this
piece of shore, although
they normally prefer sandy
or muddy stretches of coastline

I sat on a boulder to survey this desolate scene when, some four or five metres in front of me, I heard a sort of muttering and a clatter of pebbles. The next instant a dark head popped up from behind a boulder, stared resentfully at me and honked something that might have been 'Bah-Humbug'. The head was followed by its body. Two shelducks, which had been sheltering comfortably behind this convenient boulder until so rudely disturbed by my intrusion, paddled grouchily towards the sea.

Coltsfoot
(Tussilago farfara)

One of the earliest plants to flower, blooming at
the top of strong, scaly stems. The large leaves
with white woolly undersides unroll some time
after. They are very rich in vitamin C, and although
rather tough, can be used in salads. It is
always one of the first plants to take
root on new slips.

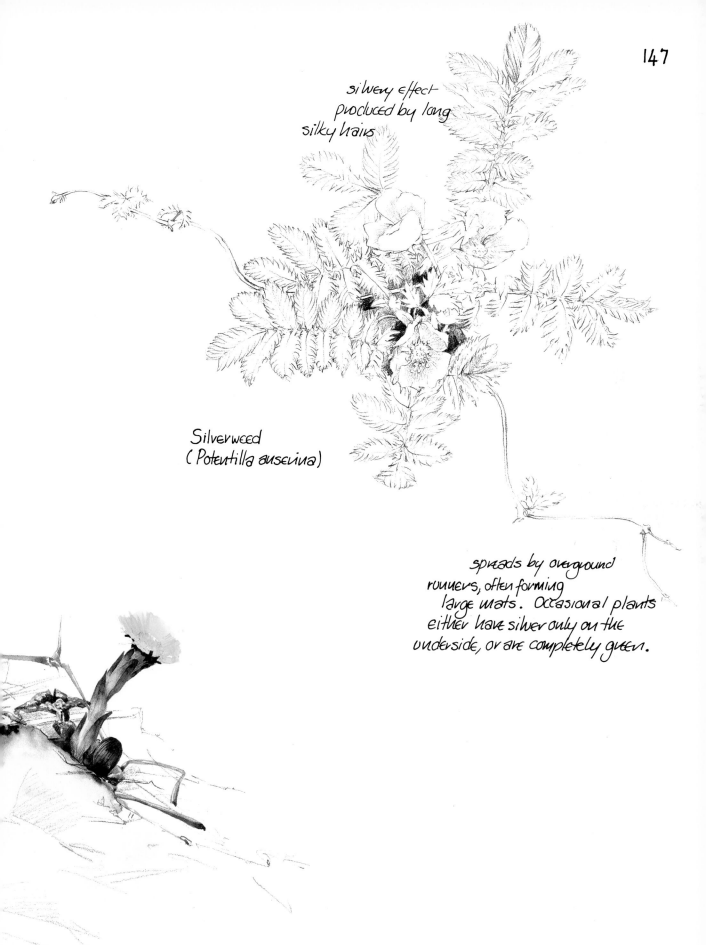

silvery effect
produced by long
silky hairs

Silverweed
(Potentilla auserina)

spreads by overground
runners, often forming
large mats. Occasional plants
either have silver only on the
underside, or are completely green.

Codlins and Cream —
Great Hairy Willow Herb (Epilobium hirsutum)
once known as 'Codded' Willow Herb — i.e.
with flowers on a stem or 'cod'.

A handsome plant stands
tall at the base of a greasy
mud-slide, its vitality a splendid
contrast to the sickly grey backdrop.
   The flower is said to have been named for its
resemblance to the red blossoms of the codlin (or codling,
as in codling moth) apple — a specific variety with long
tapering fruit. 'Codlings' was also the name given to any
hard apples used for cooking (coddling = stewing).
   This robust plant also reflects the Medieval
English meaning of its name, a
contraction of 'quer de lion' -
lionheart.

A rock pool under the shelter of a nine-foot-tall boulder contains life - a red beadlet anemone, a handful of periwinkles and, half hidden in a crevice, a long chocolate-coloured shape, a graceful finny tail sweeping the water with a lateral fish-like motion. It is an eel, its colour showing it to be a common eel, *Anguilla anguilla*, rather than the more greyish conger eel, which is also found here.

In 1963, the exceptionally cold weather resulted in the deaths of large numbers of fish that live among the rocks close to the shoreline, including conger eels ranging from 5 to 30 lb in weight. Specimens of well over 80lb are sometimes caught on lines from the beach in this area.

Centaury (Centaurium erythraea)
Very variable in size — 2in to 14in in height.
The clear pink flowers have a delicate perfume.
An annual, the flattened basal rosette develops through the autumn and winter. Flowers only open when there is sunshine.

The most common gull along this
stretch of coastline. Herring
gulls nest on the cliffs at the
western end of
the Undercliff.

Make large nests of plant
material. 2-4 eggs laid on alternate
days, incubated 25-27 days,
hatching at 2-day
intervals

The chicks grow fast, nourished on food
regurgitated by their parents. Ever
hungry, they peck at the red
spot on the parents bill, so
stimulating the adult to
deliver. With the
messy diet and pecks from
other chicks, the young gulls can become quite
scruffy around the head.
    About four weeks after hatching, the young gulls
start to use their wings, flapping and jumping
up and down, they strengthen the muscles
that will soon take them into the air and
away from the nest site.

red spot on
adult's bill

Sub-adult in 3rd winter,
still shows traces of speckling
on forewing and tail, but
otherwise has adult plumage —
bill now yellow (mottled
brown for first 2 years).

vertebra here completely exposed —

Dolphin corpse — smells appalling but the flies are enjoying it.

lifesize vertebra from dolphin corpse (scrubbed before being drawn).

head seems to have had 'beak'; approx. 8' from head to tail, therefore probably Delphinus delphis, but so far gone, it's difficult to tell.

Much other debris around — stranded jelly fish, 11" diam., clear with glass blue/green tinge. Broken crab pots, rope, net, floats and pieces of what was once a small boat.

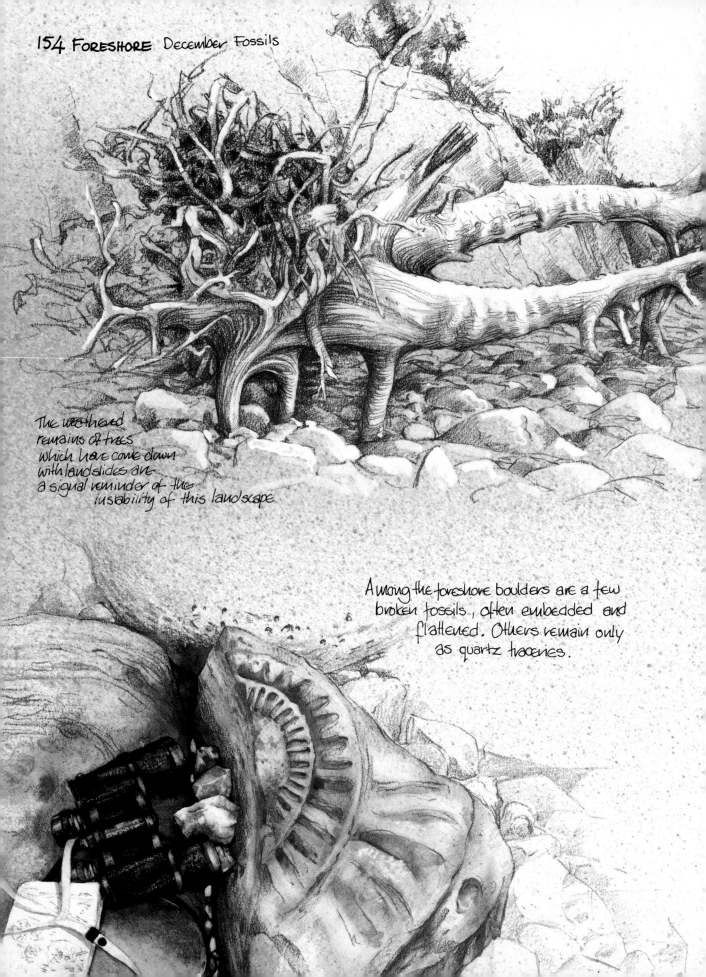

The weathered
remains of trees
which have come down
with landslides are
a signal reminder of the
insobility of this landscape

Among the foreshore boulders are a few
broken fossils, often embedded and
flattened. Others remain only
as quartz traceries.

This large example shows a section across an ammonite's chambered structure.

Both ammonite and belemnite belong to the same class as present-day cephalopods, such as the squid and nautilus. They were sea creatures feeding on small shell fish and shrimps, which they caught in their tentacles and chewed with horny beaks.

51 cm in diameter

The bullet-shaped belemnite fossil was the creature's internal skeleton or guard.

Cross-section shows radial symmetry

guard

sandstone riddled with small worm holes & burrows. — many white calcareous tubes, perhaps made by serpulid or 'keel' worms.

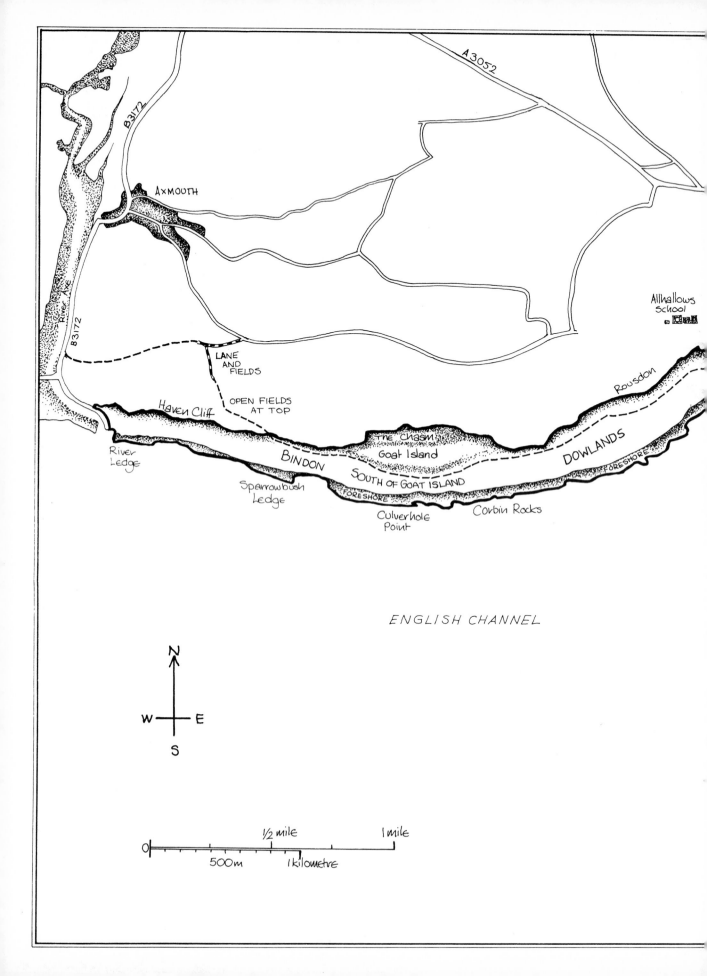

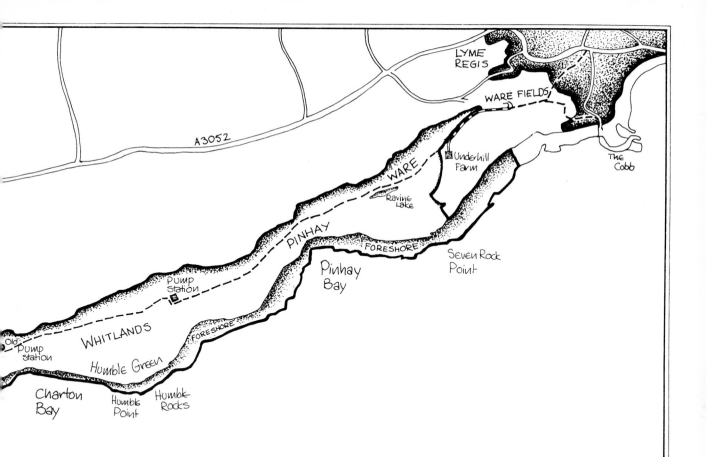

You are welcome to visit the Undercliff, but please remember it is a National Nature Reserve where serious work is done; it is not a public open space. It is all slipping; there are dangerous fissures, often hidden by undergrowth, and the cliffs and ridges are unstable.

Do not leave the public path. There are no public paths to the main road or the beach. Permission to leave the public path or to collect specimens must be made in writing to The Regional Officer, Nature Conservancy Council, Roughmoor, Bishop's Hull, Taunton, TA1 5AA, U.K.

Don't light fires, and remember, picked flowers drop no seeds, so don't destroy them; leave them for others to enjoy. We hope you will want to help us look after this unique ash woodland.

Norman Barns
Warden

BIBLIOGRAPHY

A View from the Cliffs, the East Devon Heritage Coast, edited by Richard Butler, Devon Books, 1986. Although only partly about the Axmouth-Lyme Regis Undercliff, this contains a useful bibliography of the area.

Landslips near Lyme Regis, by Muriel A. Arber, Vol. 84, *Proceedings* of the Geologists' Association, 1973. Reprinted by Serendip Books, Lyme Regis, 1976 and 1986. Also with bibliography.

Ten Plates comprising a Plan, Sections and Views .. etc., by the Rev. W. D. Conybeare, revised by Professor Buckland, John Murray, London, 1840. This is the classic first account of the 1839-40 Landslip; unfortunately a rare book, unreprinted.

An Historical Survey of the Landslips of the Axmouth-Lyme Regis Undercliffs, Devon, by J. Pitts. *Proceedings* of the Dorset Natural History and Archaeological Society, Vol. 103 (1981); and the same author's *The Recent Evolution of Landsliding in the Axmouth-Lyme Regis National Nature Reserve*, DNHAS, Vol. 105 (1985). Offprints available at the Lyme Regis Museum. The papers have extensive bibliographies.

The Book of the Axe, by G. P. R. Pulman; various Victorian editions from 1841, the best (of 1875) reprinted in facsimile by Kingsmead Reprints, Bath, 1969 and 1975. Though this covers a large area, it remains the best source for the Devon villages neighbouring the Undercliff (see Chapter xv).

The Axmouth-Lyme Regis Undercliffs National Nature Reserve, by T. J. Wallace, Allhallows School, 1966. A new edition is in preparation.

Memoirs of a Smuggler (the life of John Rattenbury 1778-1844), Sidmouth, 1837; reprinted 1964.

J.F.

ACKNOWLEDGEMENTS

I am most grateful for help and advice from Miss Muriel Arber, and Mr. K. R. Moore of the Geology Department at Allhallows School, Rousdon; and above all to Mr. Norman Barns, the Honorary Warden of the Undercliff, and undoubtedly the greatest living authority on it. Further geological information is available at Allhallows School.

J.F.

I would like to record my warmest thanks to Norman Barns, the Honorary Warden of the Reserve, for the enormous benefit of his time, knowledge and experience; also to James Kennard of the Nature Conservancy Council; to Una Greenhalgh for providing me with specimens, both dead and alive; Kelvin Boot of the Royal Albert Memorial Museum, Exeter, for allowing me to work from the museum's natural history collection; and Fiona Mackenzie, Andy and Ruth Tait for their help and encouragement.

E.F.

INDEX